FROM BOTTISHAM TO BARCOMBE

Carol Reeve

FROM BOTTISHAM TO BARCOMBE
Copyright © Carol Reeve 2006

ISBN 978-184426-398-1

First Published 2006 by.
UPFRONT PUBLISHING LTD
Peterborough, England.

Printed by Copytech UK Ltd.

Carol Reeve

FROM BOTTISHAM TO BARCOMBE

A CHILDHOOD JOURNEY THROUGH THE SECOND WORLD WAR

CAROL REEVE

Carol Reeve

Chapter One
In The Beginning

Bottisham is a quiet, straggling village halfway between Cambridge and Newmarket, with "The White Swan" at one end, "The Bell Inn" at the crossroads in the middle, and the highly praised Bottisham Village College (built in 1936 at a cost of more than £15,000) almost on the outskirts, on the way to Lode, Quy and Anglesey Abbey.

In the Domesday Book it is called Bodichessam. According to Mr. Kingston, the historian of *The Civil War in Anglia*, King Charles the First slept in this village on the night of 28 April, 1646. The previous day, shaven and with his long hair cut, disguised as a servant and carrying two bags, he had fled from Oxford. On this day, disguised as a clergyman, he had ridden from Wheathampstead to "a village seven miles from Cambridge" where he slept the night, departing next day by water to Downham.

The Parish Registers date back to 1561, and in 1931 the population rose to 649.

At the time of the Great War, the villagers of Bottisham had been cared for by Dr. Wood, but one day he suffered a tragic and fatal accident. Trying to start his ancient car with the starting handle, it had suddenly moved forward and run over him. His brother-in-law, Dr. Octavius Ennion who lived in Burwell, bought Dr. Wood's practice, thereby increasing his own responsibility to nine villages.

Dr. Ennion served in the Army throughout the Great War, and arrived home from Gallipoli, wounded but unbowed, having left all his kit behind except for his greatcoat, inside which was tucked a small brown and white terrier that had been born on the hospital ship. He also brought home two presents for his wife, Nellie - a large copper and brass urn that was thought to have been used as an incense burner, and a monogrammed leather shell case which is still in use as an umbrella stand.

The family was relieved and delighted to have him home. His son Eric was newly qualified as a doctor, though he would much have preferred to go duck shooting in the fens, or to fill dozens of notebooks with fast, accurate and indefinably beautiful sketches of birds. His unique talent to paint and draw using the simplest of strokes, and later his many books filled with affectionate descriptions of the fens and its wildlife, made his sister Ruth feel that her own attempts to paint and draw were quite worthless, and it would be fifty years before she allowed her own considerable talent to emerge.

But Ockie was far from well. He never told Nellie, but he was suffering from angina - in those days there was no alleviating drug. He began to plan his retirement, designing a single-storied house to be built in a large meadow by the river Lark in Barton Mills. It was agreed that Eric and his small family would take over the Burwell house and practice, but in the meantime he decided to take on a locum, and he knew just the man.

During the War he had met a young Polish doctor who had studied at the Middlesex Hospital in London, and who had recently taken British nationality. His naturalized name was Albert Francis Gilbert, but everyone called him Dick.

Born in Warsaw on 10 May 1895, Dick would never disclose his original name. He was almost certainly Jewish, although he denied it all his life. He was only 5 feet 7 inches tall, slim, dark-skinned, handsome, charming, and a very plausible story-teller. He claimed to have Polish, Russian and French ancestry, that one of his great-grandfathers had been elected King of Poland, and that he could speak fluent English, French, German, Polish and Russian, and while in the desert with Lawrence of Arabia, had learnt to speak and write in Arabic.

He took part in camel races across the desert, and one night woke up in his tent to find a hyena hungrily consuming his ration of cheese from his bedside table. He recounted this and other stories whenever he had a captive audience, so when his daughter Carol was about ten years old, she drew several pictures to illustrate the camel racing, the cheese-eating hyena and other tales, painted them in watercolours, and whenever Dick began, "Ah! I remember when I was in the desert with Laurence of Arabia…" she would quietly hand round her paintings without comment.

Dick spoke with the faintest hint of a Polish accent. He always stood when a lady entered the room, kissed her hand, pulled back her chair, deftly removing her coat whilst enquiring after her husband's health and totally overwhelming her with his deep-brown eyes. He was an excellent dancing partner too, and taught his little daughter the waltz, tango, foxtrot, the Charleston and even how to jive all round the drawing room. He could play his strange black mandolin, but not very well, singing "Hotcha chornia, hotcha strasnia". But he desired more than anything to be accepted as an honourable English gentleman.

The evening that Dick arrived at Harlech House, he was told that unfortunately Ruth was ill upstairs in her turret bedroom, where she liked to sleep on the open veranda regardless of the weather. He would not be able to meet her for several days. Undeterred, he bounded up the stairs, found her room and smiled down upon her.

"I am so sorry you are not vell, Miss Ruth," he said, "I hope you vill be better soon."

He bowed and went downstairs. Ruth made a remarkable recovery: she appeared in the dining room in her best frock before the dinner gong had stopped reverberating!

Some months later, during a walk up to the Newmarket gallops to watch the racehorses training on the Heath, Dick proposed marriage, and Ruth shyly accepted.

★ ★ ★

"Larksmead" was duly finished, and Ockie was taken over to Barton Mills to inspect it and admire the new carpets. But the strain was too great. He was told to rest, which meant staying in bed for at least six months. But early in 1928 he died.

Ruth was devastated. She and her mother left Burwell and moved into "Larksmead", where they sadly prepared for Ruth's wedding to Dick planned for 19 September.

Eric and Dick agreed to divide the entire practice between them, Eric in charge of Burwell, Swaffham Prior, Reach and Exning, and Dick responsible for the inhabitants of the Wilbrahams, Fulbourn, Teversham, Quy, Lode and Bottisham, where Dick bought almost an acre of land, thanks to the generosity of his friend, Octavius Ennion.

Dick's meadow had belonged to Farmer Towler of Tunbridge Farm, who kept the foxhounds for the local Hunt in a small compound with high railings from which they clamoured to escape. Mr. Towler's cows provided the family with fresh creamy milk which he measured into their enamel jugs with long-handled scoops, while the cows steamed and shuffled in the milking parlour behind.

As soon as the contracts were signed and sealed, Dick took possession of his land by manhandling a Romany caravan, that someone had lent him, across the grass and down to the shelter of a row of great elms beside a stream. Here he came whenever he could, sitting for hours on the caravan steps designing his garden – spacious lawned walk-ways between massive colour-filled borders; a sunken tennis court; an alpine and heather rock garden nestling around a stone pond that would house several generations of frogs.

At the front of the plot he drew a crescent gravelled driveway with brick pillars topped with concrete balls at each entrance, and within the curve he was to plant dozens of roses, picking a fresh bud every morning for his lapel.

He decided to balance his garden by creating a large swimming-pool on the side of the garden away from the tennis court. Finally, behind the elms, an orchard of apple, plum, greengage and cherry trees, leading into a well-stocked vegetable garden and soft-fruit enclosure.

Satisfied with his garden plan, Dick next designed his house. It had eighteen rooms on three floors. The spacious drawing room overlooked the garden on three sides through multi-paned iron-framed windows, and a French window that opened onto the terrace. Rich rugs would be scattered on the light oak parquet floor, and there would be a gilt mirror on every wall.

This lovely room graced one side of a wide wood-panelled entrance hall, heated by solid radiators of the very latest design. On the other side was the dining room, where Dick and Ruth would sit at opposite ends of the large mahogany table, and the maid would be summoned into the dining room as if by magic, thanks to Dick's clever invention – a concealed bell under the carpet by his foot. Dinner party guests were greatly impressed.

Just inside the kitchen hung a row of cow-bells, labelled "Dining room", "Bedroom One", "Nursery", "Surgery" and so on. They joggled furiously and loudly when small fingers pressed the buttons on the wall in each room. The kitchen had a large scrubbed wooden table, built-in cupboards, and a yellow Aga cooker that never went cold. Beyond the kitchen was the scullery, with its big, round washer heated by a fire underneath, where all the household washing was boiled, then taken to be rinsed in a stone sink, before being mangled and hung out to dry in the hedge-enclosed yard near the back door. There was also an ice-cool larder, with its long marble-topped shelf that Dick acquired from a mortuary. Here dozens of eggs from hens scratching in the orchard were preserved in liquid isinglass packed into brown stone Ali Baba jars.

There was a small cold toilet in a corridor outside the back door, for the servants, and opposite, a store-room filled with bags of potatoes, flour, sacks of corn for the chickens, and shelves of tinned and bottled fruit.

At the side of the steps leading to the back door from the drive was a large garage for the doctor's automobile, and in a corner of a concrete yard was the matching outsize dog kennel, complete with an upstairs shelf and always filled with clean straw.

Of all the hiding places that Dick had unwittingly incorporated into his designs, this was by far the best, because a dog will never give you away.

Chapter Two
The House That Dick Built,
1927

The front of the house was impressive, with its gabled and small leaded windows, large porch, and red-tiled steps leading up to the big oak door with its shiny dolphin knocker. At the far end of the wood-panelled hallway was the door to the garden, and beside that a door at the top of daunting stone steps that led down to the cellar. Here apples from the orchard were ranged on newspaper-covered, wooden shelves, and several times a year the concrete floor would be submerged under several feet of water. Crouching in silence on the cellar steps, Carol and her brother David would watch as frightened little mice swam in frantic circles, their black beady eyes searching frantically for refuge.

The doctor's consulting rooms formed the front section of the house next to the drawing room, behind a large, mirrored door. There was an outer entrance for patients (or "bodies" as Dick called them) at the top of the flagged path leading from the road, with two bell pushes, marked "DAY" and "NIGHT"; but it was only the bravest, most desperate body who would dare to press the "NIGHT" bell once the doctor had gone to bed.

The Waiting Room was lined with wooden chairs, and several small pictures of camels. Next door was the Dispensary, a tiny room no bigger than a broom-cupboard, crammed to the ceiling with glass-stoppered bottles, earthenware jars and empty medicine bottles. There were drawers full of different sized corks, labels, dressings, boxes of pills and powders; on a shelf near the wash basin was a Bunsen burner for heating samples, and under the narrow window a chair where the patient sat and waited while the doctor concocted yet another bottle of his miraculous, all-curing, thick, cloying, pink physic.

The final room in this annexe was the Consulting Room, with a hard, cane-covered couch, filing cabinets, shelves of regimented *World Books* next to *Diseases of Women* with its lurid colour photographs of suppurating wounds and deformities. On the doctor's desk stood his telephone. In the early thirties, Mrs. Howlett at the village Post Office worked the manual exchange. There were initially four essential phone numbers – Bottisham One was the Jenyns up at the Hall, Bottisham Two was the local police station, Bottisham Three was the doctor and Bottisham Four the Vicarage. Mrs. Howlett shared everyone's problems, gave advice on their ailments, passed on the latest gossip, and took messages if the number required was not answering. The doctor often phoned Mrs. Howlett before going out on his rounds with a list of his whereabouts, so in an emergency she could despatch the policeman on his bike, or a farm-hand on horseback, to waylay the doctor between visits.

Within a few years, owning a telephone was considered almost as essential as owning a car, but only for the wealthy farmers and comfortable property owners. Everyone else still had to walk or cycle to the doctor's surgery, no matter how far or how inclement the weather.

On the first floor of the house that Dick built there were five bedrooms, one to become the nursery. Ruth painted a frieze of Beatrix Potter characters all around the walls, and Mrs. Tittlemouse and Squirrel Nutkin adorned the chest of drawers and the wardrobe. A big rocking horse called Fancy filled one corner of the room, and he and Carol would rock for hours, flying across mountains and oceans, escaping from witches, fiery dragons and wicked stepmothers. On winter nights tucked up in her little bed, she could watch the firelight flickering on the ceiling as the embers died in the grate behind the curved brass fender, where her vest and morning socks were warming beside a spare nightie "in case of accidents". She would clutch the corner of her eiderdown and suck it as she fell asleep. Nursie was continually sewing on new patches.

All the rooms led off a wide landing at the top of an elegant staircase, and along one wall hung an enormous oil painting of the Great Fire of London. Terrified horses dragged a blackened fire tender past burning houses with women and children leaping from flame-filled windows, their cries drowned by the rattle of wheels and thudding hooves, and over all the acrid smell of smoke. This painting disappeared during the war years and was replaced by a boring landscape with cows, and no-one remembers what befell the Great Fire of London.

Next to the bathroom and small toilet was the walk-in airing cupboard, with wide slatted shelves stacked with bed linen around a warm tank – an ideal place for a cat to give birth to her kittens or where a small girl could hide from an avenging brother.

A small door opened onto a steep staircase leading to the attic rooms, where the maids would sleep on flock mattresses, their porcelain chamber pots under their beds, and large jugs on the wash stands for carrying water from the kitchen to fill the china bowls.

The view from these attic windows across the meadows and cornfields to the rookeries in the Park was unforgettable. It was from these windows that the family were to stand and watch the sky burning red as London suffered another great fire, in the Blitz, sixty miles away.

The house was built during 1927, with dark rustic bricks that had been removed from a derelict Nunnery. This gave it a curiously weathered and elderly appearance, so that passing tourists would often stop to photograph the "stately home" which Dick christened Beaulieu House – a truly beautiful place. Once the furniture had arrived from Harrods, Dick moved in and began to work on the garden. He was approached by a young man whose parents lived a few yards away down the Swaffham Road, with an offer to help in any way he could. Arthur Wisbech became gardener, handyman, chauffeur, and eventually the children's dearest friend and confidant. "Wizz-wizz" was the only person who knew all the secret hiding places in the garden and in the house, but he never revealed them.

★ ★ ★

It was Wisbech who drove Dick over from Bottisham to his wedding at Barton Mills on Wednesday, 19 September 1928. Dick was too nervous to drive himself, perhaps not altogether surprising after his hurried visit to London earlier in the week to spend his last bachelor night in the arms of an unidentified lady friend.

So at a quarter past two, Ruth Ennion married Dick Gilbert at St. Mary's Church, Eric giving his sister away, while his little daughter Sheila proudly carried the bride's train. Ruth laid her bouquet on her beloved father's grave in the churchyard. The weather was sunny and warm so tea was served on the front lawn of Larksmead in the shade of the big chestnut tree, and the couple left for the first night of their honeymoon at a hotel in Market Harborough. On the way they suddenly realised that with all the excitement they had eaten very little and were now starving, so they stopped for a meal in Cambridge, hoping that none of their wedding guests would have the same idea and see them.

Ruth knew nothing about the sexual needs of men on her wedding night, only that it would be her duty to surrender her virginity, whatever that might mean. But Dick was caring and gentle, and the honeymoon passed happily enough.

Being used to living in a doctor's house, with all its commitments, Ruth settled down easily to the job of being the wife of a doctor with a large country practice. She took his messages for him, wrote out the bills, and with the help of Mrs. Howlett, would recruit the local policeman to track down the doctor and give him a list of recent calls. Her first task was to interview suitable applicants for the position of cook and housemaid, who were to "live in" and perform all the household duties except planning the menus.

★ ★ ★

The young doctor and his wife were eagerly invited to many dinner parties, so Ruth had to organise her own. Their circle of friends widened, and soon the parties at Beaulieu House became an absolute must for the gay young things of the County. All through the summer, couples sprawled about the garden, sipping Dick's special cocktails in between loud games of tennis, and after dinner they danced on the lawn to strangulated foxtrots from the wind-up gramophone.

Winter parties usually included the games of Murder, or Charades, or word games and quizzes. But the Pirate Party was the talk of society for months. Arriving suitably dressed at the front gateway, guests were confronted by a ferocious brigand (Wisbech) who demanded their invitation cards or their lives, before he would show them where to park their jalopies. Dead-Eye Dick greeted them in the hall, and they were ushered into the drawing room, which was now furnished entirely with bales of hay.

Eventually all the lights were turned off, everyone dispersed around the house, and there was much giggling and appeals for mercy in the darkened bedrooms until someone was "murdered". Then the lights came on and everyone was expected to remain perfectly still (except the "murderer") while the "detective" viewed the "body" and then called for an inquisition in the drawing room. On this occasion, all the guests were blindfolded, and pieces of the victim's body were handed round to be felt and identified: his eyes (peeled grapes), his intestine (a string of sausages) his liver and kidneys. Hot toddies were served in pewter mugs, everyone became very merry and eventually departed as dawn broke.

★ ★ ★

Ruth had always been a keen Girl Guide having started as a Rosebud even before Brownies were invented. She set up a Girl Guide pack in the village, and Dick became Scout Leader. The Guide Commissioner, Marguerite de Beaumont, became a very close friend, attending their dinner parties, admiring the extensive garden with Dick; he was captivated by her elegant bearing, her deep voice and her witty, tantalising conversation.

Their affair was very discreet and was never mentioned by anyone in Ruth's presence, but Ruth was fully aware of her husband's infidelity, and accepted that this was inherent in his European blood, and it was her duty to stand by him, for better or worse. Besides, she was expecting a baby. Marguerite eventually went away to live in Wiltshire, where she bred horses. She never married.

On 8 October 1929, Adrian David Francis Gilbert was born in the big walnut bed at Beaulieu House. Dick brought his own son into the world, and Ruth later wrote: "David was a perfect baby, healthy and lovely, no trouble, so I used to wonder why people found motherhood so difficult and tiring". A young girl from Fordham, near Soham, came to live with the family as David's Nanny – Kathleen, always known as Nursie, Palmer. David was a plump, happy baby, with big brown eyes, a mass of tight blond curls and dimples in his cheeks.

Two years later, Carol arrived. Her mother wrote: "Carol was born on 14 December, 1931, a wee baby and always crying". Captain Bert Rumbelow was her godfather, and Marguerite de Beaumont one of her godmothers. The other was a spinster friend of her grandmother – Olive Howard. She had been engaged to a nice young man, whom she took to introduce to her widowed mother. They got on so well that he decided to marry the mother instead. Some years later, when her mother died, Olive went to stay at her stepfather's home as his housekeeper. She devoted the rest of her life to him. In her will, she left Carol a beautiful jewel-encrusted ring; she often wondered if it had been given to Olive on her hapless engagement.

Carol was christened at Holy Trinity Church, Bottisham by Reverend Utthwatt and howled throughout the service. The population of the village had now increased to 649.

Chapter Three
Early Days, 1931

During her first summer, as she lay in her pram watching the leaves playing with the sunlight, Carol's special guardian would be lying nearby, apparently asleep but alert and ready for action. His name was Christopher, and he was a golden retriever.

The Gilberts' first dog had been a little wire-haired fox terrier called Rex, who trotted round the tennis party guests and yapped at their ankles. He adored Dick, and would watch from the bedroom window for his return from visiting his patients. One day he became so excited that he jumped through the open window and died at his master's feet. So Christopher came to join the family soon after David arrived.

Mrs. Gilbert would be arranging flowers or answering the telephone when Christopher would bound in from the garden and stand in front of her, tail at half-mast, ears cocked, and a worried expression on his face. Then he would lead her back to the pram and its yelling occupant. He continued to look after Carol as she learnt to crawl and then toddle, clutching his thick fur for support.

★ ★ ★

The doctor and Wisbech began to work on the new swimming pool, marking out the perimeter, and then organising the massive task of excavating hundreds of tons of soil, with the help of a borrowed digger and several local farmhands. The finished pool was about ten feet wide, two feet deep at the shallow end with four steps, and the floor sloped away to six feet and rose again to five. This made it safer for diving.

The floor and walls were covered with cement and painted a bright cornflower blue. Concrete slabs around the edge helped to keep the grass at bay, but there was always a bowl of water by the steps to encourage everyone to wash the grass-cuttings off their feet before entering the pool.

The doctor would tie a child's fishing net to the end of a long bamboo pole with which he could sweep up the dead leaves, floating twigs and drowned beetles from the surface of the water at least twice a day, and more often during the autumn. It would take at least two days to fill completely through a hosepipe attached to a tap outside the kitchen window, but emptying it was a Parish triumph. The pool needed cleaning out once a year, the floor and walls scrubbed clean to get rid of the green slime, then the cracks had to be filled and the whole interior repainted. But first the water had to be emptied – doing it by the bucket-load would have taken months, and with a small electric pump almost as ludicrous. The answer lived further up the road, in a shed behind Freddie Potter's builder's yard. This was a Coventry Climax, a petrol-driven engine that could pump water from flooded coal-mines or village ponds, and was kept in readiness by the village firemen but it rarely saw regular service and they had very little practice in fire fighting.

Freddie Potter and his men would tow the machine up the drive, and then manhandle it round the side of the house between the hedges, and line it up beside the pool. A long tube with a basket on the end would be put into the water, the engine started up and the fireman would brace themselves with the hose pointing away from the house.

Suddenly a great jet of water would shoot out, and the crows nesting in the elms would be forced off their perches. The tennis court, the flower beds, the rock garden would all be drenched, and so would most of the village children who had crept into the garden to watch.

★ ★ ★

Swimming parties became even more popular than tennis parties, and in particularly hot weather and especially at weekends, car loads of acquaintances and young people on bicycles would arrive unannounced, to be followed by Eric and Dorothy Ennion with their three children, the Turner family from Cambridge with their six children, the five Pendreds from Swaffham Bulbeck, and the new vicar, Harry Russell, and his daughter Joan. They all wore tightly fitting rubber swimming caps, uncomfortable hand-knitted bathing costumes that reached down to their thighs, and even the men wore all-in-one costumes with matching belts. When neither the family nor friends were using the pool, the housemaid and Nursie ventured in for a swim.

Nursie Palmer had beautiful bright eyes, rosy cheeks and an infectious giggle. When Carol was new, she slept in the nursery, and her meals were brought up to her there. Later she was invited to dine with the doctor and his wife, and she recalls that they treated her with affection, and as a dear friend of the family. She was the first person Carol saw every morning, the one who bathed her, dressed her, played with her, read stories to her about Peter Rabbit, the Flopsy Bunnies, Little Black Sambo and the tigers who melted into butter, and Peter Pan and Wendy. She nursed David and Carol through chicken pox, mumps and measles. Before the discovery of the triple vaccine, parents would hold special Measles Parties so that a child confirmed with having the disease could pass it on to as many others as possible.

Nursie wheeled Carol in the deep black pram with removable floorboards into the Park, David and Christopher walking beside them, and she introduced the children to cows, cowslips, frogs, kittens, birds, pixies, other babies and Good Manners. Nursie introduced them to the local shopkeepers too. The men in the street would touch their caps and say "Mornin', Miss Carol, mornin', Mas'er David!" while the women gave them a polite nod.

The children loved to stand in front of the blacksmith's forge watching the sparks fly as the hammer clattered onto the hot horseshoe, shaping it to a perfect fit. Their faces red and glowing in the heat of the wood fire, they would draw in their breath as the smithy tucked the horse's leg between his knees and nailed the horseshoe home. The big horses never flinched as the smell of burning hoof sizzled in the air.

Nursie often took the children to watch the baker, Mr. Coleman, working in his bakery on the corner of Bell Road, putting newly-risen dough in shining metal tins into a huge oven, and lifting out the cooked ones with a big palette, helped by his sons Maurice and John. Groceries were ordered from Mr. Bedford, and on Sunday mornings the children and Nursie went to the Sunday school in the church; if they behaved nicely, sometimes the children were allowed to pump the handle that made the organ come to life. Carol liked that, because up in the gallery behind the wooden casing of the organ, no-one could see her and she did not have to pretend to pray or sing.

At Easter and Christmas their parents came to church too, and they all sat in their own wooden pew with a little door. The Jenyns family, who owned the Park and lived in the spacious Hall, had a superior pew so enclosed that it was like a small stable, and no-one could tell if the inhabitants were awake or asleep, or even if they were inside at all.

★ ★ ★

One hot summer's day, when Carol was about eighteen months old, she was playing tea-parties with her Teddy on the lawn, giving him pretend sips from a little tin teacup, one of a set laid out on a stool. Nursie still insists that she was away that day, visiting her family in Soham, or "it would never have happened!" But someone who was supposed to be keeping an eye on her was dozing in a deckchair nearby, and was quite unaware that Carol had decided to fill the teapot with real water. So off she trotted to the swimming pool.

Carol knelt down by the steps and watched the water rush into the pot so fast that she let it go and it began to sink. She reached out to catch it – and fell in, head-over-heels. She could see a cloud turning very slowly above her in the deep blue sky. She floated gently round in a circle, the skirt of her little smocked dress filled with precious air, keeping her afloat. Just like Eeyore, playing Pooh-sticks.

David, aged three, had been watching. He ran to the occupant of the deckchair, shook her awake and announced with pride, "Cawol's in the 'wimming pool!" How she must have screamed! Within seconds, their father tore out of the house, plunged straight into the pool and lifted Carol to safety. She did not start to cry until everyone else did.

As she grew older, she hated the swimming pool, hated her cousin Hugh because he could swim under water, and hated her brother and all his friends who splashed her mercilessly. When she was about eight years old, still refusing to venture into the water further than the steps, her father decided to prove to her that water was fun. He picked her up and threw her into the pool. She sank, struggling for breath, terrified that she was going to drown. Somehow she touched the floor of the pool and managed to drag herself out and ran indoors. She never lost her fear of drowning, and still felt hurt that her father should have acted so thoughtlessly and so cruelly to her, his darling little girl.

★ ★ ★

About the time of that first unpleasant encounter with the swimming pool, the family acquired two goats, Blanche and Nanette, who munched the long grass and rotten apples in the orchard, and provided the children with fresh warm milk.

There was general concern at the time that cow's milk caused Tuberculosis unless it was pasteurised, and until pasteurisation became obligatory, the doctor insisted that they only drank goat's milk.

In 1935, Blanche took part in a special Parade to celebrate King George V and Queen Mary's Silver Jubilee. The village was decked with flags, the pavements lined with smiling faces, when Blanche strutted along the High Street pulling a small Swiss cart in which Carol sat like the Queen of the May, with Wisbech proudly acknowledging the admiring cheers at Blanche's head.

May Day was another special occasion, when Carol dressed her doll Rose in her best clothes, laid her in her little pram, and covered her with daisies. Nursie decorated the rest of the pram, and together they walked up Swaffham Road to the High Street and up Bell Road, accepting pennies from everyone they met, and finishing their journey at Wisbech's house for tea and some of Violet's delicious scones.

★ ★ ★

Carol stood in the driveway of Beaulieu House one afternoon, waiting for the new Mayor of Cambridge to pass by. His car slowed down when he saw children at the side of the road, and he threw out handfuls of coins, which they scrabbled for the moment the big limousine pulled away.

★ ★ ★

A curious event took place during a long weekend at Southend-on-Sea, where the family went to stay with Uncle Shah and Auntie Mabel, a sister of Granny Ennion. In the corner of their small garden was a little wooden sunhouse, and Carol was sitting there with her mother when they heard a loud bang, followed by a terrible scream from the road outside. The doctor grabbed his medical case and rushed out to see if he could help.

The horrified driver of an open tourer explained that her husband was sitting in the open dicky seat at the back of the car, when it had suddenly snapped shut with him still inside! The poor man was quickly released and laid out on the verge to recover.

The high point of that weekend was going for a ride on the tram that clattered along a tree-lined central reservation with roads on either side. It was much more exciting than the children's roundabout on the beach, which made Carol dizzy and did not go anywhere.

★ ★ ★

Frequent visits were made to Burwell to see the cousins, and they often came over to spend a day at Bottisham. Their Nannies were good friends, so while they sat and gossiped, the children played adventurous games. Sheila was usually rather bossy, so the others avoided her as much as possible; while David and Juliet caused chaos in as many ways as they could, Hugh and Carol pedalled their tricycles or fought over their respective toys.

One of the children's favourite and most daring adventures together was to do the Attic Run. The slope of the roof created a narrow triangular passage that ran all around the house behind the maids' bedrooms. This narrow gap was thick with dust, huge spiders and occasional mouse droppings, and it was completely dark. It was however just wide enough for children to crawl around. One day they attempted the Attic Run without a torch, dared on by the cousins, and they all emerged at the other end absolutely filthy, their clothes ruined and with cobwebs in their hair. Auntie Dorothy was far from pleased.

A few days later, David and his closest friend Graham Brown, followed by a very reluctant Carol, tried the Attic Run once more. Suddenly in the pitch darkness, Graham crashed into something solid with sharp horns – a stag's head complete with antlers that someone had jammed across the passage.

Their screams were heard by Nursie, but no-one ever owned up. It must have been put there by someone tall enough to lift down the stag's head from its hook in the hall, and who knew that this would be the best way to make sure the children never dared to attempt the Attic Run again.

Uncle Eric (was it he?) was always beaming, always interested in whatever the children were doing, and he could draw wonderful pictures. His beautiful artistry was to be recreated in the landscapes of his son, Hugh. Of all her grandchildren, there was no doubt that Granny Ennion's favourite was Hugh, though she tried to treat them all equally. Juliet rejoiced in being the naughtiest, and caused the maid Doris much annoyance on one visit to Beaulieu House by grabbing hold of the toilet roll in the upstairs loo and walking downstairs and out into the garden dragging it behind her. When the house was full of noisy children during a birthday party, either Wisbech or Doris would be given the onerous task of keeping Juliet and David well apart, preferably in different rooms, or some dreadful prank would ensue.

Punishments were always carried out in those days, and were accepted without question by the offender. It ranged from a quick slap on the leg, to being sent to one's room without anything to eat until their father appeared early in the evening with his cane. David felt the cane more often than Carol did: waiting for Daddy to come was punishment enough, and she usually received a stern warning followed by a warm hug. Her most persistent crime was to stick out her tongue at Doris when she asked Carol to do something she hated, like eating up her greens.

★ ★ ★

Mrs. Gilbert learned to drive a little Austin 7 in the thirties, and she would take David and Carol over to Barton Mills to see Granny Ennion. Sometimes they stayed overnight, and Carol would wake to the cooing of doves in the big dove-cote that Ockie had commissioned.

The house was full of photographs of their grandfather, and of Ruth and Eric as babies in stiff frocks with lace collars, and recent photographs of all her grandchildren; and everywhere oil paintings of lions and deer, painted by an uncle, Bouverie Roberts, and several drawings by Eric.

Granny was looked after by her maid Gertie, who slept in a room under the eaves, and had a fascination with dressing-up. She would nearly always be waiting on the steps of the bungalow when the family first arrived, dressed in a long black satin dress, a black lace shawl, black mittens clutching a Dorothy bag, and with a white cap covered with black lace, just like Queen Victoria on Granny's Jubilee mug in the kitchen. She even adopted a special wheedling voice, and the children were a little frightened of her, despite the sweets and toffees she produced from the depths of the Dorothy bag. She reminded them of the witch in Hansel and Gretel. But once she was dressed as Gertie the maid, with her blue dress and white linen apron and cap, Carol was quite happy to scrape out the pudding bowl before tea.

★ ★ ★

One summer, when Carol was still quite small, they were invited to the house next door to Larksmead, where there were crowds of people attending an afternoon party. The house belonged to Sir Alexander Fleming, the scientist who first grew penicillin in his laboratory, and it was a privilege to have met him. Carol spent the entire afternoon swinging in the hammock in his garden.

Another day, Granny took David and Carol to Mildenhall station to watch the steam train come in, and the driver invited the children onto the footplate. The engine rumbled slowly down to the buffers, then back onto the crossing points, gathering speed as it steamed out of the station and away towards Cambridge. Carol began to cry, but David wanted to go faster. However it soon slowed, and ran backwards to join up with the waiting carriages in the platform, and Granny.

★ ★ ★

Nursie took Carol on the train to spend a weekend at Soham with her family when she was about five. It was harvest time, and they were carried to the fields in big wagons pulled by shire horses. There they helped to pile the sheaves of corn into stacks – Carol searched and searched, but could not find a needle – and they picnicked with Nursie's brothers and the other labourers. That night Carol slept in a wide bed under a white coverlet, and discovered that the shiny knobs on the brass bedhead unscrewed quite easily.

The next morning she was taken to see an old black carriage with long shafts and tiny windows, which was kept in the yard behind the house. It smelt very musty, but Carol was lifted inside and she felt like a princess riding to a ball.

But she was no princess, just a pale freckled child with red hair - and she was about to go to school.

Chapter Four
Peace For A Time, 1937

In 1937 Carol was taken to St. Colette's Preparatory School near Cambridge railway station, where David was already a pupil. There were no pre-school or play-groups then to accustom a child to such a strange environment, but that first morning she was allowed to sit at the back of the top class, presumably to give her time to adjust. The teacher and the pupils all ignored her. It was not long before tears welled and the pain inside her could no longer be controlled. She sat in utter misery, soaking wet from her underwear down to her shoes and socks, with a puddle widening on the floor below. Someone eventually noticed, and drew the attention of the teacher, Miss Randall, as well as the rest of the class. Carol felt humiliated and ashamed. Her brother was utterly disgusted with her, and she just wanted to curl up in a corner and die until Wizz-wizz came to take them home at four o'clock – and then more misery, when the change to borrowed clothing had to be explained.

In time, Carol began to like going to school. She made several friends, most of whom invited her to their parties. In return, her parents joined with others and threw a huge tea party at Christmas time for everyone, in an upstairs room at the Dorothy Café in Cambridge. Tea dances were held in the ballroom downstairs; a trio or quartet played waltzes, quicksteps and foxtrots while older people took tea and watched from little gilt chairs as young couples danced and fell in love – all with the utmost decorum and perfect gentility, of course.

At the age of six Carol fell in love with Michael Chapman, who was five. He was a pale, quiet little boy prone to being bullied, so she became his shadow and protector. She knew about bullying – at home her brother tormented her whenever he could, and it usually culminated with her teeth sinking into his arm or leg, David screaming for help, and both of them being punished. But one day at St. Colette's, a boy pushed Carol to one side quite deliberately. David squared up to him, his face red and angry.

"You leave my sister alone!" he shouted. "No-one pushes my sister around. Don't you ever do that again or I'll... I'll..."

He was wonderful, and she said so. But he immediately told her to shut up and go away.

St. Colette's was run by two sisters, Miss Burns whom the pupils all feared, and Miss Beryl whom they all loved. The school was a single-storied wooden hut with wide verandas where they took their lessons in good weather, and with a playing field nearby, at the end of a short lane. They learned to recite their multiplication tables until they knew them all up to twelve-twelves without having to concentrate. Most of the children could read before they were six, and they all took part in the school sports day and the Christmas Nativity play.

Christmas was special for Carol – the new King, George VI, was also born on 14 December, and flags would fly from civic buildings on their birthday. But he had never enjoyed any of his birthdays as a boy, having had the great misfortune to have been born on the anniversary of the death of his grandfather, Victoria's beloved Albert, and everyone wore black and looked solemn on that day.

At the end of her first Christmas term, Carol was chosen to be one of the angels in the Nativity play. They had to wear flimsy pink tunics with matching pink knickers. When they arrived at the ADC theatre to change into their costumes for the performance in front of hundreds of proud parents, Carol discovered that Nursie had packed her tunic but not her knickers. Nursie was already in the audience and Carol had to go on stage before she could find anyone to help her. She stood on her box, with the other angels, mortified that everyone would see that she was not wearing anything under her tunic.

They sang *O Come All Ye Faithful* at the end, every verse word-perfect and in Latin.

★ ★ ★

The following summer holiday of 1938 seemed, at first, to be as carefree as they had always been, although Carol missed her Nursie who had gone away to look after her brother's family. The Gilberts motored down to Cornwall, stopping at Stonehenge for lunch, and Tiverton for tea, and spent two weeks with the Turner family in their house "South Corner" near the cliffs of Treyarnon Bay. While Robin and David dashed into the mountainous waves, Lindy and Carol searched for small creatures in the warm rock pools left behind when the tide went out, or lay on the clifftop bravely watching the angry sea crashing below them into unseen caves.

★ ★ ★

Back at home in Bottisham, Carol spent as much time as possible in the garden, helping Wizz-wizz to find the eggs, or pull up the sweet young carrots that tasted so nice when he had cleaned them for her on his handkerchief. Close to the tennis court was a green and white painted summerhouse, constructed on a circular rail so that it could be pushed round to face the direction of the sun. Under the bench inside were stored the rackets, plimsolls, and clock golf equipment, and when she was younger, Carol's fully equipped dolls' house that looked remarkably like her own home.

A few feet away stood a gnarled old tree, with wide splayed branches, and the doctor and Wisbech built a Wendy house for the children that just fitted snugly within its arms, and they nailed a ladder in place up to the front door. It had windows at each side, with curtains, and inside a small square table in blue with two matching chairs. Carol spent much more time up there than David, drawing, writing stories, or playing "mothers and fathers" with Joan Russell, the Vicar's daughter, who was the only friend she had living in the village. Joan was considered a "suitable" companion. However, Carol much preferred to play with Bernard, Wisbech's son who was the same age as her and never argued, and let her sit on his lap on the swing. This was reported to Mrs. Gilbert by Doris, and after that Carol was no longer allowed to play with Bernard, because he was "unsuitable".

The tree house became Carol's refuge from Doris and the rest of the world; she shut herself in there when David was massacring the rooks with his air-gun. He took a pot-shot at Freddie Potter's little terrier one day and the poor dog bolted up the road yelping in pain, but David made sure Carol did not tell anyone. His best friend was Graham Brown who lived in a large house called The Grange right at the end of the village, near the White Swan inn. He had three brothers, Malcolm, Puck (Carol's favourite) and little Bruce. David and Graham had a plan, and they actually allowed Carol to share it. They spent all their pocket money on as many sweets and bottles of Tizer as they could carry from Millard's shop up the road, and they stacked boxes of liquorice sticks, twists of sherbet, bull's eyes, and chocolate bars inside the tree house. They each had their own store, and agreed to save everything for, literally, a rainy day.

But alas, while Graham was away on holiday, David and Carol gave way to temptation and ate all their own stocks, and then embarked on Graham's, all of it, washed down with Tizer. They were both extremely sick, which helped to appease their sense of guilt. Graham of course, was furious when he called round, and refused to have anything more to do with David and Carol – for several days, anyway. If only they had foreseen the years of sweet rationing that lay ahead, their secret hoard would have been an Aladdin's cave!

★ ★ ★

One morning, as she sat in a corner of the kitchen chewing one of Christopher's dog biscuits, Carol heard Doris discussing her wages with Cook.

"It's not right," she was saying, "I get ten pence an hour for doing all this work, washing up, cleaning, emptying the slops, polishing the surgery, cleaning up after that little Madam – and Elsie up at the 'All is getting eleven pence an hour an' she only 'as the old lady to do for!"

Carol went and told her mother and Doris got her rise. Her workload, however, was about to be considerably increased.

★ ★ ★

Over lunch the doctor tried to explain as simply as possible that Herr Hitler in Germany had threatened to invade Austria and Poland, unless he and our Prime Minister, Mr. Neville Chamberlain, could come to some sort of an agreement. Meanwhile hundreds of refugees were already leaving their homes and coming to England to be safe, and families were being asked to take one or two refugees into their homes.

"So tomorrow Frau Silbermann from Vienna, her mother and daughter, will be coming to stay with us, and I want you to be very polite to them. We thought we would convert the nursery into a bed-sitting room for them, and put the mother into your room, David."

Both the children were upset. Carol's things were moved into the spare room at the front, and David had to squeeze into the only other bedroom on the first floor. Doris grumbled and muttered to herself, as displeased as the children.

The following day, the doctor fetched the Silbermann family from Cambridge. The children watched the car turn into the drive, and stood well back as three ladies clambered out of the car. They were all dressed in black, clutching brown paper parcels and carrier bags, which they put down in the entrance hall before embracing Mrs. Gilbert fervently, weeping and exclaiming, "Danke – danke viel grusse!" David and Carol escaped rapidly.

Doris brought China tea with lemon slices, and thin slivers of toast spread with anchovy paste, to the drawing room as usual that afternoon. The doctor spoke German well, so he was able to learn more about the Silbermann's predicament.

"Mr. Silbermann is dead," he translated, "but they did manage to bring one or two things out of Vienna, and these will be arriving at Cambridge in a few days."

The three ladies were so overwhelmingly grateful that they insisted on helping in the house. Frau Silbermann took over all the cleaning and dusting, Margrit waited at table, and the old lady helped Cook prepare the meals. Within days, Doris had had enough and gave in her notice. She marched off down the drive to Carol's great satisfaction.

A few days after their arrival, a large van pulled up at the door, and Wisbech helped the carrier unload a massive cabin trunk, two large wooden crates, and finally, with great difficulty, a tall white-painted object that turned out to be an over-size kitchen cabinet. It had cupboards at each end, two smaller ones in the middle, glass fronted shelves and a long row of tiny drawers, each one labelled and still containing an amazing variety of herbs, spices, coffee beans and rice. Room had to be made for this monstrosity in the kitchen, where it was discovered that the cupboards were crammed full of tablecloths, sheets and towels.

The big trunk containing their clothes was taken upstairs, but Margrit opened the crates and scattered straw and crumpled newspapers all over the floor. Soon every inch of space was piled high with soup plates, cups, saucers, teapots, vases, a complete dinner service, sherry and wine glasses, and several porcelain figures. Margrit handed one to Carol – a white parrot with a golden beak, standing on a golden ball.

"For you!" she said, with a big smile. David said it was a German eagle, but he was jealous, of course. How the three refugee women managed to escape from Vienna with all these heavy items was never revealed.

The upheaval was too much for Cook, who took her wages and left like Doris before her.

The Silbermanns were now in total command in the kitchen, and Carol was immediately commandeered to do the dusting and polishing, and David was shown how to tidy his room, fold his clothes and shine his shoes. The children even assisted with the washing-up for the first time in their lives, and Mrs. Gilbert quietly undertook any other job that kept her out of sight – darning, letting down hems, and spending long hours in the garden pruning and cutting flowers, consulting Wisbech, and writing long letters to her mother in Barton Mills.

Fortunately the Silbermanns preferred to spend the evenings in their own rooms, so after Surgery the family could sit together and listen to the wireless, relieved when they heard that Mr. Chamberlain had flown home from meeting Adolf Hitler in Germany with a piece of paper in his hand, announcing "peace in our time".

Long before the Gilberts might have become accustomed to German food heavy with herbs and garlic, the Silbermann family decided to move into a flat in Cambridge with some Austrian friends, so they packed up their china and porcelain and departed. But they left behind the huge kitchen cabinet. This pleased Mrs. Gilbert, but now she had to fend for herself in the kitchen, and she had never cooked a meal in her life. Fortunately, Nursie's mother came over from Soham to help, and two of the doctor's patients who lived in the row of white-painted cottages across the road, offered their services: Mrs. Pettit, a gentle little person, and Mrs. Cornwall who could make the most delicious rich, buttery scrambled eggs imaginable.

The family had plenty of eggs from their own chickens, and grateful patients often paid their medical bills with sides of pork, or lamb chops, plump ducklings or geese ready plucked, freshly churned butter, cream, cheese or duck eggs. This continued the tradition of Grandfather Ennion, who often came home from visiting his patients in the Fens with a chair, or table, or an ornament, which had "taken his eye".

Granny Ennion's housemaid, Gertie, had to be certified in 1938, and was sent to a mental hospital in Fulbourn. Granny regretfully decided to sell "Larksmead", and she came to live in a rented house in Bottisham, just a hundred yards away from Beaulieu House. She insisted that the children visited her every day, in particular on their way to Sunday school. But most Sundays their parents were far too busy to remember, so when they failed to turn up, Granny would march up the drive to take them herself. As soon as they heard her boots crunching on the gravel, David and Carol would rush upstairs and hide in the attic until they were found out, or more often, until Granny gave up and stomped home.

Granny Ennion had a repertoire of useful sayings: if anyone should accidentally burp or, worse still, break wind, she would say: "Beg your pardon, Mrs. Hardin'."

She would ask a question, and if the children took rather a long time formulating the answer, they knew what she would say:

"And answer came there none, and that was scarcely odd because they'd eaten every one."

Carol puzzled for years about this curious statement, until she discovered that it came from Lewis Carroll's *The Walrus and the Carpenter*.

Two of Granny's sisters also decided to move to Bottisham, into another detached house almost across the road from Granny's; Auntie Totty from Sussex, and little Auntie Mabel who had "lost" Uncle Shah somewhere in Southend. Auntie Totty was the eldest of the three, a sedentary and rather awesome lady who lent Carol two books to read – "What Katy Did" and "What Katy Did Next". These impressed her deeply, because she always liked to jump off her swing when it was high in the air, like Katy did, but so far she had not broken her back and been forced to lie in bed for months, learning to be Patient and Good. Auntie Mabel kept house for them both, straightening the hand-woven mats that nestled in every doorway, and knitting underwear for Carol's doll, Rose. Carol became very fond of them both, and missed them greatly when they passed away before the end of the War.

★ ★ ★

Once a week David and Carol were taken to the Corn Exchange in Cambridge for ballroom dancing lessons. He hated them more than she did, and made himself so unpleasant that their parents were asked to remove him.

Carol eventually progressed to ballet classes with a sweet lady called Sally Bicknell, but her lanky arms and legs, knock knees and flat feet, were not designed to emulate a graceful cygnet floating on a lake.

David and Carol were given piano lessons too, by an endless procession of exhausted tutors, but Carol could never stretch an octave with her crooked little fingers.

"Witches fingers," David said. "Like Anne Boleyn."

Carol complained bitterly when the last teacher rapped her on her knuckles with a ruler. Their piano lessons finally ended when the old piano was wheeled out and put on a cart, with David, Bernard and Carol sitting beside it, and as the horse plodded along the lanes to Swaffham Bulbeck, they took it in turns to thump the keys. Carol even managed to play the only piece she ever learned, *The Jolly Farmer*.

A few years later, the doctor bought a smart new upright piano that matched the parquet in the drawing room, and only special guests were allowed to play upon it.

★ ★ ★

David and Carol went to see their first pantomime, *Dick Whittington*, at the historic old Festival Theatre in Newmarket Road, long since demoted to being a furniture warehouse. Their first film was *Snow White and the Seven Dwarves*, and Carol was more upset by the huntsman than the wicked Queen, because he killed a defenceless little fawn and presented its heart to the Queen to make her think Snow White was dead. The only other film that affected Carol more deeply was *Dead of Night*, in which a ventriloquist's dummy slowly turned into its Master.

The family were lucky if they ever saw the end of a film, because invariably a hand-written message would appear on the screen to their intense embarrassment: "Would Dr.

Gilbert please report to the foyer where there is an urgent message for him."

They would stumble over invisible legs in the darkness in their haste to leave. The doctor had no partner to share the workload of the practice, so he had to notify Mrs. Howlett at the telephone exchange beforehand and tell her which cinema or theatre they were intending to visit.

★ ★ ★

The children both loved reading, but listening to Children's Hour was essential. The Toy Town characters were Carol's friends – Larry the Lamb, Ernest the Policeman, Mr. Growser and Dennis the Dachshund who spoke in a thick German accent. Uncle Mac not only read the stories and played all the parts, but he introduced most of the other programmes as well. He seemed to speak to Carol personally so she sent him a story about a rabbit, and he actually wrote back to thank her. Bedtime was never far away when Uncle Mac brought the broadcast to an end with the gentle words "Goodnight, children – everywhere."

Chapter Five
Digging In, 1939

Easter 1939 became memorable due to Carol's throat becoming so sore that she could not swallow anything. Tonsillitis was diagnosed. Her father drove her that afternoon to the Evelyn Nursing Home in Cambridge, where she was left alone in a tiny room on the first floor, with a window overlooking the garden. Suddenly she heard the fire escape rattle below her windowsill; someone was grunting as they clambered up. A boy of about twelve peered in at her and said, "Hallo! What are you in for?"

"Tonsillitis," she gulped.

"Oh, right," he said, climbing in and sitting on the edge of her bed. "It's not very nice, tonsils, but you'll be all right – you'll see!"

A nurse hurried in and her new friend jumped up. "Just going!" he said, and clambered out through the window and down the fire escape. The nurse closed the window with much tut-tutting and "Well I never did!" and told Carol to go to sleep. She never saw the boy again. To a little girl only seven years old he was Peter Pan.

Back home, with a throat like red hot cinders, Carol could swallow nothing but ice-cream for weeks. David was very sympathetic and ate all her chocolate Easter egg as well as his own so it would not be wasted.

During the summer of 1939 it became increasingly likely that there was going to be a War. Despite Mr. Chamberlain's peace pledge, the British people were preparing themselves for the worst. The doctor brought home some cardboard boxes containing a gas mask for each member of the family – a suffocating black rubber thing with a pig-like nose that tied at the back of one's head, with a little cellophane window that misted over when one tried to breathe. Everyone was told to carry their gasmasks with them wherever they went, once War was declared.

The doctor had designed an air-raid shelter, and supervised Wisbech in its construction. It was several feet deep and wide enough for five or six people to sit on benches on either side. It had a tin roof covered with all the tons of soil that Wisbech, with David and Bernard's help, had dug out of the ground, and grass seed was sprinkled all over the top. It was close to the surgery door so the patients could get to it quickly as well as the family. Unfortunately it suffered from the same problem as the cellar, and several feet of water had to be emptied out with buckets before Wisbech managed somehow to resolve it. Blankets were kept down there, some tins of biscuits and lemonade, and Carol often hid in the shelter when there was a particularly boring job waiting to be done in the kitchen.

Bread from the local bakery was delivered daily by young Maurice Coleman, the baker's eldest son, and there was always a special twisty loaf for Nursie. A lot of giggling and teasing used to be heard when Maurice was hovering at the back door, so no-one was surprised when they became engaged, and the wedding was fixed for 14 August 1939.

★ ★ ★

At school, a large part of the grounds of St. Colette's was now covered by a square concrete shelter, and every day, in the middle of a lesson, Miss Burns would blow her whistle and the children would close their books, line up, and march out to the shelter in complete silence. They had to stand there for ten minutes, then march back. Should the real siren ever sound, they all knew exactly what to do.

They duly carried their gas masks everywhere. To make them look less ugly, they covered their boxes with Christmas wrapping paper, or pieces of dress material, replaced the string with coloured ribbons, and stitched or painted their initials on the back. They were also given an identity number which they had to learn, and Carol never forgot hers – TBHY 215-4.

★ ★ ★

Carol was very proud to be asked to be Nursie's smallest bridesmaid. She was fitted for her full-length mauve and pale blue dress, and stayed the night before the wedding in Nursie's home. They were married in the parish church at Soham, and after the ceremony Maurice gave Carol, and the older bridesmaid, a little gold bracelet.

They went to live in a small house in Lode, near enough for Nursie to call on the family until her first baby was born. Carol cycled over to see him when he was a few weeks old, and she cried all the way home because she knew she had lost her Nursie.

Then one day Wisbech collected David and Carol from school and gently told them that their dear old dog Christopher had died that morning. Carol was utterly bereft and miserable. Nursie and Christopher had been her dearest friends all her life, and now they had both deserted her.

A few days later the doctor brought home a small brown and black puppy, a Border terrier. "This is your dog, Carol," he said. "She belongs to you." Carol was overjoyed, and hugged and kissed her new friend. She decided to call her Peggy.

On 1 September, they heard on the wireless that Poland had been invaded by the Germans, and the effect on the doctor must have been devastating, although he never showed his anguish to David or Carol, and kept the truth from them. Hundreds of Polish families had been dragged out of their homes by the Nazis and hanged on the trees outside. He could only guess what terrible fate had befallen his own relations.

Two days later War in Europe was declared. Everyone had been expecting it for so long that it was almost a relief. At school the children sang the new words to *Under the Spreading Chestnut Tree*.

"Under the spreading chestnut tree, Neville Chamberlain said to me,

'If you want to be a VIP, join the ruddy LDV'."

Wisbech explained that VIP meant Very Important Person, and LDV were the Local Defence Volunteers, a group of men who were either too old or too young to join the Forces but would guard their villages and homes. Doctor Gilbert decided to set up a platoon in Bottisham.

Carol asked Wisbech if he was going to be called up to join the army to fight the Germans, but he hurriedly changed the subject, not wanting to have to explain to her that he was a conscientious objector. But he would volunteer to play his part working on the land.

★ ★ ★

Carol's best friend at St. Colette's was Lindy Turner. Their mothers had become close friends, and remained so throughout their long lives. Carol loved going to their big house on Huntingdon Road at Girton, where she tried desperately to attract the attention of Lindy's eldest brother, Robin, but all in vain. Lindy was a superb pianist even then, but no-one would ever have dreamed that she was destined to become the wife of an Archbishop!

In 1949 Mrs. Turner took all six children to America "for the duration", leaving their father, Professor Bunt Turner, to continue teaching law at Trinity Hall. The doctor and his wife decided to send Carol and David to the

States as well, and a home was offered to them in Connecticut by a Miss Starr. Carol was not at all happy at the thought of leaving the only place she knew, her friends, her little Peggy and her parents; in fact she burst into tears and said she would not go. But Miss Starr sent a long letter describing her house, the forests and lakes nearby, the skiing in the mountains, and with it she sent a photograph of her little white Sealyham puppy. Perhaps it was not such a terrible idea after all.

The doctor took David and Carol to London to the Passport Office and to the American Embassy. There was a long queue of people waiting for visas, and it was several hours before all their documents were completed, signed and stamped. Then they went to buy two large suitcases, a blue one for Carol and a brown one for David, around which their father carefully painted a white stripe one way and a blue stripe lengthwise, with their initials near the handles.

Their names were put on a very long list – so many children were waiting to be evacuated and every ship was full. Special broadcasts were arranged across the Atlantic, and one night they listened to Lindy talking to her father.

Then on 14 September 1940 news came that one of the crowded ships heading for the United States, the City of Benares, had been attacked by a German submarine and had sunk. Eighty-five children died.

Mrs. Gilbert held Carol very tightly when she told her what had happened. There was no question now – David and Carol would not be going away. The risk would have been far greater than the possibility of being bombed at home, even though London was under attack every day. Whatever happened, the four of them would stay together.

★ ★ ★

Wisbech had a wicked smile on his face as he drove them home from school one day.

"There's a surprise waiting for you," he grinned. "The village has been taken over by an army of little cockney urchins – they're tearing across the fields as though they ain't never seen grass afore, and you should 'ave seen 'em run when Mr. Towler's cows came down for milkin'!"

The evacuees had arrived clutching parcels of clothing, with labels pinned on their coats. They had no idea where they were, and while the local children stared suspiciously at them, their parents chose whichever evacuee they thought would fit in best with their own offspring, or who might provide that extra help needed with the housework.

"Have we got one?" Carol asked, and Wisbech nodded.

"Little girl called Lilian – taken quite a fancy to your tree house."

Lilian took a fancy to everything, and claimed them for herself - Carol's clothes, her toys, her paint box, even her secret hiding places. She discovered David's collection of bird's eggs and broke some, so for the first time David and Carol became allies in an undeclared war against "them" – for Lilian had brought her mother with her. Mrs. "B" commandeered the kitchen, wearing a scarf round her curlers, and smoking a cigarette. She found fault with the Aga, the tradesmen, the countryside, and especially David and Carol.

Their meal times were all wrong apparently – midday lunch became dinner, afternoon tea disappeared and they had tea at five o'clock, while their parents had supper at eight instead of dinner. Every meal, whatever it was, tasted horrible. Their fresh greens were boiled for twenty minutes until all the goodness and flavour had been lost, and anything that could be fried was drowned in fat. David and Carol were forced to eat up every last morsel, although Lilian was excused because she had a weak stomach.

Whenever a piece of china broke, it was because it had already been cracked, and it was never Lilian's fault. Poor little Peggy was "a dirty, mangy hanimal" – how Carol hated "them"! Mrs. Gilbert took refuge in the garden even more frequently, and visited Granny twice as often as before.

★ ★ ★

On Saturdays Carol went with her father as he "did his rounds", visiting his patients in all the neighbouring villages. He used to hold a surgery in the front living room of a lady's house in Great Wilbraham, though he could do little there other than listen to their complaints and hand out prescriptions and advice. Carol would wait outside in the car, and watch women filling buckets of water from the pump in the High Street and stagger home with them. Bottisham had its own green-painted pump too, near the new Vicarage, because mains services had still not arrived in the countryside, and hot running water and indoor toilets were luxuries which only the professional classes could afford.

★ ★ ★

They now had a bucket of sand in the hall, with its own trowel ready to smother any fires that might start during an air raid, and it made a very convenient ash tray for Mrs. "B".

Wisbech practised using the stirrup pump in a pail of water, working the handle feverishly up and down to raise a decent jet of water – fortunately he tried it out in the garden.

Mrs. "B" had strict ideas about bath-time.

"No baths at night – wakes you up – so baths first thing in the morning. Only two inches, mind, and Lilian gets in first." Carol was allowed to bath next, then David by which time the water was cold and full of scum. They complained bitterly to their parents, who were very sympathetic but preferred not to engage with the enemy.

Then, totally unexpectedly, Mrs. "B" announced: "We're goin' back to London, bombs an' all – I'd sooner face Hitler on me own 'ome ground than in this godforsaken dump."

Wisbech drove them to Cambridge station with their bags and suitcase, while the family whooped with joy. They celebrated with afternoon tea and anchovy toast fingers, while the doctor outlined his exciting new project – to dig up the entire tennis court and grow potatoes. The Government was extolling everyone to Dig for Victory, so Wisbech was volunteered for the job. Bernard came to help, the doctor took his turn when he could, and David and Carol forked over the soil, pulling out as many worms as they could for David's fishing trips to the stream at the foot of the cowslip meadow beside the garden.

★ ★ ★

Mrs. Gilbert became quite adventurous in the kitchen, trying out specially invented recipes for wartime cooks, and it was Carol's job to put on thick leather gloves to pick quantities of nettles which when cooked tasted very much like spinach.

Food was rationed in the shops and customers were only allowed small quantities of essential food – so many points each week – and Mr. Bedford cut out the little square coupons from their ration books when the Gilberts went to collect their order. Bartering or swapping became an acceptable way of acquiring extra luxuries: a pot of pre-war home-made jam must have been worth several yards of dress material.

Every curtain in the house had to be lined with black material so that no light could be seen from outside at night, as this would attract enemy aircraft. The smallest chink would bring the Air Raid Warden pedalling furiously up the drive, shouting "Put that light out!" He was Mr. Paul, one of the local farming landowners, over six feet tall and straight as a ramrod. It was also his duty to tell everyone if and when an air-raid was imminent, as there were no sirens in the village. He had a notice pinned to his coat with "ALERT" written on one side, and "ALL CLEAR" on the reverse, so he could turn it round when the emergency was over. To make sure everyone knew the alarm had sounded, he would blow a whistle, long and hard.

★ ★ ★

Then dear little Peggy disgraced herself by becoming pregnant. She went back to the kennels at Swaffham Prior for the confinement, but it was several days before Carol was told that she would not be coming home. "It's for the best" was the only explanation given to her. Not knowing if Peggy had been put to sleep, or had been given away, Carol presumed that she was being punished for some terrible misdemeanour of which she was unaware. She became bitterly resentful, and knew that no-one loved her.

Her father understood, and did his best to make amends. He had been told that a local farmer had been called up to join the Army and his golden Labrador, Skeet, was looking for a new home. They drove out to Six Mile Bottom: Skeet leapt all over Carol, washing her face with his rough tongue and whirling his tail round in circles. He had always lived in a stable, so they tied him up beside Christopher's old kennel that first night.

He howled. And he howled. And he howled.

Exasperated, the doctor stomped outside to admonish the dog. He returned a few minutes later with Skeet at his heels. The dog made straight for the rug in front of the fire, grinned at everyone, stretched out full length and fell asleep.

The following morning, Skeet was let out to water the garden. But he did not reappear. The family called him, looked for him everywhere, but he had disappeared. It was dusk when they heard an urgent whine outside the kitchen, and then an impatient scratching at the door.

Skeet was damp and bedraggled; he went straight to his water bowl and drank deeply. The Gilberts were told later by the local policeman that Skeet had been seen loping down the lane to his old home. He must have searched all around the farm but once he was quite sure that the place was deserted, he had decided to come back to his new family.

Chapter Six
Tank Traps, 1940

There was no warning the day the tanks arrived, just a grinding, rumbling, squeaking, crunching that grew louder and louder as the vehicles headed down the road towards Beaulieu House. Standing at the front door, Carol thought she saw a soldier's head moving along the top of the hedge, then a great grey tank appeared in the gap in the driveway, swaying dangerously from side to side as it passed.

She ran down the drive as another tank creaked and thundered past, then another and another. The air was full of dust and noise: people were running out of their cottages and waving to the soldiers in each turret. Wisbech and the doctor came to watch.

As the last tank went by, it lurched slowly to the left, swung back and took most of the brick gatepost with it. The concrete ball that had been so proudly cemented on the top lay in the road like a dirty snowball. The doctor shook his fist at the tank. He shouted something unintelligible in the clamour and, amazingly, the tank ground to a halt.

The doctor shouted again, jabbing his finger towards the dislodged segment of wall: "PUT THAT BACK!"

The soldier vanished inside his turret but shortly reappeared and climbed down. He picked up the piece of wall and wedged it as well as he could into place, then he picked up the concrete ball and balanced it on the top. With a quick salute, he climbed back into his tank and it lumbered away.

Lorries full of soldiers were now following the tank convoy and behind them dozens of village children and evacuees. Carol joined in, and they ran as fast as they could to see where they were all going. The big iron gates at the entrance of the Hall were open, and the tanks were peeling off and stopping beneath each of the big trees that fringed the park.

The soldiers were covering the tanks with huge nets dotted with coloured rags.

"Camouflage" an evacuee explained, "so that the henemy haircraft won't see 'em from the hair."

The children were moved along by a burly officer, who threatened the "scruffians" with dire consequences if they ventured inside, now that the park and the Hall had been "requisitioned", whatever that meant.

In the days that followed, whenever a tank passed Beaulieu House, more of the brick wall was smashed. The doctor complained to the Battalion's Colonel, who drove round to the house with his chauffeur. They parted on the friendliest terms, having shared reminiscences of their experiences in Egypt during the First World War, and with the promise that if the Army would mend their walls, the Gilberts would agree to billet some of his married officers and their wives. The single officers had moved into the Hall, with Mrs. Jenyns and her maid confined to two or three rooms at the back of the house.

★ ★ ★

Inspired by the sight of army uniforms, the doctor dressed up in his Home Guard outfit, peaked cap, baton and shiny brown shoes.

"Captain Gilbert of the Home Guard, at your service!" he boomed.

He allowed Carol to go with him to watch his troop drilling at Bottisham Village College. The Local Defence

Volunteers had been renamed the Home Guard, probably because it was shorter to print on epaulettes and communications. The members were all known to her, and she tried to identify them as they lay in strange positions all around the football field, with labels tied on their uniforms.

One was moaning terribly. "My right leg! Piece of shrapnel right through the knee…"Carol read his label. "It says here 'Fractured Left Elbow'.

"Ah!" he said, "Oh, my poor arm!" as a stretcher party ran up to them.

Carol followed them into the Village College, where her father explained to the stretcher party and other men in uniform, how to bind broken bones and clean wounds.

In the circular library, Carol went to stroke Fancy, her dear old rocking horse. Her parents had given him to the College shortly after it opened, and Carol had been thanked for her "generosity". She had not been consulted of course, just as no-one had explained to her why she had to give her favourite woolly black piglet and other soft toys to the "poor" of Barton Mills before Granny left.

Walking back towards the village, Carol saw Dummy in his little hut built on the grass triangle between Lode Road and Swaffham Road. He was a deaf-mute, and the boys of the village teased him mercilessly. The hut had a small one-way window rather like a cat-flap, where the villagers pushed their shoes through for Dummy to mend the next day. One evening Maurice Coleman and his friends collected twenty-one cats from around the village and shoved them, one by one, into Dummy's hut. He must have had a terrible shock when he opened the door in the morning – but Dummy bore no-one a grudge. Despite the assaults with catapults and the name chanting, he saved all the spare pennies he earned and bought the children sweets.

Carol hurried past and went into Millard's sweet shop, but she only had sixpence with her and no coupons. She pointed to a small chocolate bar. "Do I need coupons for that?" she asked. "Well, no" said Mrs. Millard, "but you won't like it, Miss Carol!"

"Ah well, I'll have it just the same," said Carol. She left the shop and ate it as she walked home. That evening she had a really bad stomach ache, and had to sit on the toilet for hours. Her mother found the wrapper in her coat pocket and gently poked fun.

"You ate a whole bar of laxative chocolate for invalids – no wonder Mrs. Millard warned you not to buy it!"

★ ★ ★

With the Home Guard preparing for an invasion and the British Army encamped in the park, the War seemed much nearer. As well as black-out curtains, windows were criss-crossed with sticky brown paper, road signs were removed or obliterated, street names blacked out and any stranger daring to ask directions would be viewed with the utmost suspicion.

In Cambridge, a large water tank with WD painted on the side had been placed on the grass in front of King's Chapel, and passers-by threw pennies into it. Many townspeople slept in public shelters at night, while barrage balloons hung overhead, their taut wires making it too dangerous for an enemy pilot to fly as low as he would have liked.

In the countryside, he had virtually no resistance. The Bottisham Air Raid Warden, Mr. Paul, had abandoned his bicycle in favour of a small car, blowing his whistle out of the window. The car was old, and the engine noisy, and during one memorable air raid he wondered why people were waving at him fiercely and pointing at the roof of his car. He continued down Bell Road blowing his whistle, but people still threw up their windows and gesticulated alarmingly. Eventually he stopped and got out to see what all the fuss was about, and looked up.

A German Messerschmitt zoomed above his head, splattering the road all around him with machinegun fire. It had apparently been dive-bombing him for some time, swooping down and going round and round again out of sheer devilment. Mr. Paul dashed into the nearest house, and eventually the pilot got bored and flew away. This story was the topic of conversation for weeks in all Bottisham's pubs as well as the surgery.

The Battle of Britain was being fought in the air daily now, and the smoke trails weaving patterns across the sky. The family listened to the news broadcasts and the sonorous voice of the new Prime Minister, Winston Churchill, praising the gallantry of the little planes.

★ ★ ★

David moved his egg collection and his clothes up into one of the attic bedrooms when his room and the nursery were taken over once again, this time by two officers and their wives. One officer also brought his batman, whose name really was Tommy Atkins. They also turned the dining room into their private sitting room, so the family had to eat their meals in the kitchen.

The Gilberts continued to entertain, the Doctor recounting his adventures to the new audience of officers, who appreciated Carol's paintings. There was one good-looking man who stood quietly on his own and Carol asked who he was.

"He is a Member of Parliament," her mother said, proudly. "His name is John Profumo."

★ ★ ★

The household consumed large helpings of potatoes which grew extremely well in the tennis court. Carol was shocked to discover that one of the rather plump wives was not keen on washing clothes – when the front of her jumper got splashed with food, she simply turned it round and wore it back to front.

★ ★ ★

David was now a day-pupil at the famous King's Choir School, Carol was due to leave St. Colette's, and Graham and Puck Brown went to the Perse School. To save on petrol coupons, the Browns and the Gilberts agreed to take turns in transporting all of their offspring to their various schools on alternate days.

At about half past eight one morning, the fog was so thick that Wisbech had to drive as slowly as he could, his eyes on the grass verge as it unravelled out of nowhere, when BANG! An RAF armoured car had crashed straight into them. The driver and his companion had been sent out to search for a German aircraft that had been shot down somewhere in the area, but were totally lost in the fog.

Carol found herself lying in the road behind the car, and one of the RAF men lifted her up and laid her on a car seat that they had placed on the grass. The Brown boys were beside her. David was near by, his face covered with blood, and beyond him in a crumpled heap lay Wisbech. Carol heard him whisper, "It's all right, Carol – just look away." Carol watched the telegraph wires swinging and swirling in the drifting mist above her, and heard an ambulance drawing up to take David and Wisbech to Addenbrookes Hospital in Cambridge.

Another car stopped – it was Madge Towler, their neighbour, and she immediately offered to take Carol and the two Brown boys to the doctor's house. When they arrived, the doctor had just left, having received a call that there had been a bad accident on the Newmarket Road. To his horror he recognised his wife's car smashed beyond repair, but no sign of any of the occupants. Distraught, he drove home to ring the hospital, and found Carol and the Brown boys shivering in the kitchen.

David's face had been deeply cut by broken glass, but he managed a weak grin when Carol was allowed to visit him a few days later, and he admired the big lump on her forehead. Wisbech was in the same ward, swathed in bandages. His broken limbs would mend well, but his smashed nose would never be straight again. When at last he was allowed home, his face was so changed that Carol could hardly bear to look at him.

While David was convalescing in his attic room, Carol was able to give him a running commentary on the devastations being wreaked on the meadow next door. First bulldozers flattened the front hedge, and then heavy lorries drove through the gap, piled high with prefabricated buildings. Gangs of men put up Nissen huts at the far end of the meadow: wooden igloo-shaped buildings with tin roofs which were to be the soldiers' dormitories. They also built a canteen, a lecture hall, a medical room and a chapel.

Nearest to Beaulieu House they built a large, single-storied flat-roofed building that had no windows and apparently no door, but it had a tall chimney. No-one seemed to know what it was for: rumour spread that it was something to do with Gas, definitely Top Secret, and it hummed constantly day and night. Fixed to the chimney was the camp's Tannoy system, which let out angry howls of alarm and made announcements that the whole village could hear.

It soon became clear that the family were not alone in being greatly disturbed by the destruction of the meadow.

While Wisbech was recuperating, it was Carol's job to feed the hens in the orchard. She would fill a pail with corn from the sacks in the outhouse. One morning she put her hand into the sack to feel for the scoop, and touched something furry that moved. There were three little mice inside stuffing themselves with corn. Later that day her mother met a mouse in the drawing room, and found mouse droppings on the stairs, in the airing cupboard and under the kitchen table. That night Carol could hear their little feet scurrying across the bare floorboards of the attic. David hid under his bedspread, but eventually switched on his bedside light and a family of mice sat up and stared back at him.

The Army wives refused to get out of bed until their husbands reassured them that there were no mice hiding in their slippers. Sadly, dead mice were found floating in the water tank in the attic, which the doctor had to scoop out and bury in the garden, and every drop of drinking water had to be boiled after that.

Eventually the mice departed as silently as they had come, presumably to the open fields beyond the orchard. One or two stayed behind and brought up their children among the warm pipes that connected the radiators throughout the house. Carol looked on them as small casualties of War, evacuees in fact, and much preferred them to the cockney variety.

Wisbech knew what to do. He brought a small grey kitten to be Resident Mouse Catcher, although it was far too young to be trained. David insisted that it should be christened, so a moving ceremony was held in the garden, David wearing one of his father's loose collars back to front, and holding a fruit bowl full of water. Carol held the squirming kitten while David patted its forehead with water and pronounced,

"I baptise you Mr. Perkins."

Unfortunately in a very short time Mr. Perkins disputed his name and became fat and heavy with babies. This fascinated the doctor who insisted on being present at the birth, which took place in the hut used as a changing room by the pool, and he actually delivered five tiny kittens. Within minutes, Mrs. Perkins' natural instinct to reject human intervention forced her to dispose of her contaminated first-born – by eating them.

The doctor was dreadfully upset and pretended to David and Carol that they had died at birth, but eventually confessed what had really happened. He was banned from any future confinements.

Mrs. Perkins produced five kittens regularly three times a year for the duration of the War, usually in the airing cupboard in a specially prepared box, but occasionally somewhere in the garden. She would carry them indoors one by one, by the scruff of their necks, and lay them in her box. Poor Wisbech had the onerous task of drowning the unwanted progeny – the idea of having Mrs. Perkins spayed was never even considered.

In between her pregnancies, Mrs. Perkins became Carol's cat, sleeping on her bed, greeting her from school, listening to her imaginary adventures, and sharing all her secrets. But no-one can recall that she ever caught a mouse.

Chapter Seven
Out Of The Blue, 1941

Before the War, the Gilberts would go to Treyarnon Bay in North Cornwall for their summer holidays, sharing the Turner's house "South Corner". But Britain's beaches had become out of bounds, occupied by concrete posts and metal posts jutting towards the sea, and land mines hidden beneath the sand to hinder any invasion. Barbed wire ringed the coastline, blocking the footpaths to everyone.

However they did take a holiday one summer in the early years of the War. The Ennions had bought a caravan which occupied one corner of a large field near Stoke-by-Nayland in Essex, and Auntie Dorothy insisted that the Gilberts make use of it, offering Uncle Eric as a locum to look after the Bottisham practice as well as his own – as she said, "After all, it's only ten minutes drive away."

Anyone else took at least twice as long to drive the five or six miles between Burwell and Bottisham along narrow, twisting lanes, but both Eric and Dorothy ignored all corners which saved a considerable amount of time. They never slowed down and only stopped if they caught sight of a bird – an emergency stop, both feet hard on the pedals, field glasses up to the eyes and a rapid identification of the bird's species, sex, age and size. Uncle Eric often drove along the roads following the flight of a bird through his binoculars, steering the car with his elbows and his knees. Dr. and Mrs. Ennion never seemed to be involved in accidents, perhaps because they were happily unaware of the crumpled vehicles strewn behind them that had been forced to take drastic avoiding action.

It was agreed that Mrs. Howlett at the telephone exchange would intercept Dr. Gilbert's calls and transfer them all to Dr. Ennion.

★ ★ ★

The car was packed with bedding, crockery, tins of food, games, spare clothing, Skeet, children and their parents. They waved goodbye to Mrs. Perkins who was left in charge of the Army wives, and, after several wrong turnings down country roads where all direction signs had been removed to confuse German spies, they eventually spotted a grimy caravan propped up at the end of a sloping meadow beside a thicket of blackberries.

While Mrs. Gilbert swept out the cobwebs and grey cocoons from the caravan, her husband began to dig a shallow pit near the blackberries, placed a bench with a hole in it over the top and put up a striped canvas windbreak discreetly round three sides with the opening painfully close to the brambles. He then hung a small bunch of newspaper squares over the end post by a looped string. It was certainly private, but not exactly convenient.

Skeet, David and Carol explored the meadow, picking the creamy mushrooms that grew everywhere, and then at the top of the hill, stopped in amazement, staring at a double-decker bus. It was embedded in a tangle of grass and nettles, weeds eating up the floorboards. Not an ordinary bus but an old-fashioned, rusty, open-topped one with outdoor staircases at either end, curving down to the platforms below. David and Carol spent the rest of the day "driving" it, collecting tickets and ringing the bell.

That night, after a good wash in fresh stream water, Carol slept well until she found herself on the floor being given the kiss of life by an anxious Skeet. Her mother tucked her back into her bunk, and then at three o'clock she fell out again. David was told to swap bunks with his sister, and she slept peacefully. At five o'clock, David crashed onto the floor.

They realised in the daylight that the caravan was not level, so spent the morning collecting stones and shoving them under the caravan's wheels. In the afternoon they all went for a long walk, accompanied by a robin's wistful piping in the hedgerow, with sightings of kestrels, skylarks, thrushes and clusters of chirpy sparrows. The War seemed a million miles away.

That night the Germans launched their biggest raid on London. They heard the artillery first, and then watched the searchlights pinpointing the droning bombers in the vast black sky. At times the meadow seemed to shake as bombs thudded into the ground just a few miles away. The supporting stones shifted under the caravan. The raid went on all night; the family huddled together in blankets watching the flashes of orange and green, and slept fitfully, cold and afraid but together in safety.

In the morning they realised that the caravan had tilted more precariously than before. They decided to manhandle it a little way down the slope to a more level site, so they kicked the stones away, but had to jump clear as the caravan trundled downhill by itself, coming to rest with its wheels buried in a low bank, inches from the stream. Then the skies opened, transforming the field into a bog, and as the stream began to rise towards the caravan, they decided to pack up the car and drove gratefully back to Bottisham.

They found the Army wives trying to relight the Aga. It was lovely to be home!

★ ★ ★

A few weeks later, the tanks emerged from the park and rumbled away, followed by the soldiers in trucks and jeeps, the officers and their wives. The Gilberts had the house to themselves again. They flung open the windows, stripped the beds, emptied out the smelly ash trays, reorganised the furniture and ate their lunch in the dining room once more.

But then it was time to send David to boarding school at Oundle, his new uniform and cricket whites packed into a large trunk, and Carol pretended she was glad to see him go until the car disappeared out of sight. At least she had Skeet and Mrs. Perkins to look after; and then Wisbech came back, sadly changed but still her dearest friend and comforter.

★ ★ ★

While the camp-site next door was unoccupied, the women of the village met once a week in one of the Nissen huts, to talk while knitting socks, woolly hats and long scarves for the Forces. Carol went too, with her mother and Granny Ennion, and was given a never-ending pile of worn black socks to darn. The ladies gossiped about babies, how to make puddings with dried eggs, and speculated about the future of the camp-site. Rumours spread that it was going to become a prisoner-of-war camp for Germans, or perhaps a hospital for the wounded.

But men in blue uniforms had been spotted digging in a field on the main road, opposite the end of Bell Road, so Skeet and Carol went to investigate. There was now a wide concrete road right across the field, and Bernard said it was an air-strip. The RAF was coming to Bottisham.

Returning home, they found a tall man in RAF uniform talking to the doctor in the rose garden. He had gold braid on his hat. He saw Carol staring, swept his hat off and pointed to the braid.

"Scrambled egg," he explained, and introduced himself. "Squadron Leader Harold Pound, at your service, ma'am".

He gave a deep bow, and Skeet washed his face. Carol hoped he was going to be billeted with them, but he had come to offer three of his nicest officers.

"I am putting them in your sole charge, ma'am" he continued. "You will have strict instructions to report back to me should they fail to clean their teeth or polish their boots."

Carol ran to tell Wisbech, but he had other things on his mind. He was watching a heap of rubbish smoking in the corner of the vegetable garden, poking it now and then with a stick until little flames darted into life. He took her hand and told her that now he had recovered from the car accident, it was his turn to be called up.

But it was against his conscience to kill other human beings, so instead of joining the forces, he was going to work on the land.

"Ploughin', harvestin', whatever they arsks me to do, so I'll be doin' my bit for ol' England, see."

The smoke stung Carol's eyes. Wisbech promised that Bernard would help in the garden after school, and she could look after the hens and collect the eggs.

"One day I'll be back, you'll see – large as life an' twice as natural!"

When Carol and her mother went upstairs to begin preparing the bedrooms for their new visitors, they saw Wisbech from the landing window. He was standing in the distance under the elms, leaning on his spade, and gazing across his beloved garden.

★ ★ ★

One of Carol's first RAF responsibilities was Pilot Officer Ginn. He was very quiet, preferring to stay in his room than sit downstairs with the others. They nicknamed him Pink Ginn. Carol's friend Joan Russell, the Vicar's daughter, suggested that they might cheer him up a bit if they made him an apple-pie bed. The girls tucked the bottom sheet in as usual, then folded the top one in half and turned it down so that it looked properly made up. Carol tried to stay awake that night, waiting to hear his shouts of laughter as he tried to get into bed. But she heard nothing. The next morning she smiled conspiratorially at him over the breakfast table, but he just looked at her, cold as ice, and said not a word. He obviously had no sense of humour.

* * *

Although the camp-site was very large, so many of the officers had brought their wives and children with them that cottages had to be found for them to rent in Bottisham and the surrounding villages. After school, the garden at Beaulieu House would be filled with the sound of happy children splashing in the swimming pool, while their mothers sunbathed in deckchairs near by.

Dr. Gilbert decided that a tennis court was far more beneficial than a potato field, so he organised parties of off-duty officers to pull up all the potatoes, clear the weeds and rake the soil. Then they took it in turns to drag the heavy roller up and down the entire length until the doctor was satisfied that it was really flat. They scattered bags of grass seed all over the area, while Carol and the other children played at being scarecrows and banged saucepan lids to keep the birds away.

While he waited for the tennis court to mature, the doctor designed a small golf-course around the rest of the garden, fraught with natural hazards like rose bushes and steep slopes, with holes just the size of tobacco tins dug into the ground, each with its own little flag. It was a great success. Wisbech would have been appalled.

The swimming pool had become very dirty and slimy, and in great need of being emptied and then cleaned. The doctor had a brilliant idea – he telephoned Squadron Leader

Pound and told him that the house was on fire. Within minutes, the camp fire tender was hurtling up the drive, the men piled out and began unfurling pipes to take water from the pool.

"Where's the fire?" shouted Poundie to the little group of fascinated onlookers.

"What fire?" Carol shouted back. Her father was smiling.

"Just my little joke!" he said, "To see how quickly you chaps could go into action. Very impressive. So, while you're here, you might like to have a go at emptying the pool – jolly good practice, what?"

Poundie was not at all amused. He gritted his teeth. He took a deep breath and then ordered his men to pack up and return to the camp. As soon as they had left, he began to tell the doctor what he thought of his "little joke", very loudly and distinctly, before marching off down the drive.

Carol and her father cleared the leaves and slime as best they could, and the doctor put chlorine in the water to kill the germs. Families still came to swim whenever the sun was shining and no-one complained at all. But Carol still sat and watched them from a safe distance.

★ ★ ★

Soon tennis matches were being played again. Despite the rationing and the dismal news on the radio, Bottisham seemed to be isolated from the outside world – until the Alarm screamed from the tower next door. Poundie said it was called a Tannoy because that was its job – to annoy. The officers would dash away, dragging their uniforms on over their swimming trunks, and not long after, the roar of engines could be heard as the little planes took to the air.

The children learned to recognise the different types of planes from their engine noise – German bombers whined and throbbed between two notes, while our bombers hummed on one continuous note. Sometimes they stood watching line after line of bombers going over the house towards Germany, with their fighters surrounding them for protection. Later they watched them returning - those that did return. All too often the doctor would receive a phone call, and Carol would know from the expression on his face that one of their friends would not be coming back.

The Gilbert Family

Ruth Ennion   Dr. A.F. Gilbert

Olive Howard with Nellie, Ruth, Dorothy and baby Sheila
Ennion at Burwell

Beaulieu House, Bottisham, with Christopher

The Garden of Beauleiu House

Carol and David with Nursie Palmer

Carol and David with Wisbech

Cleaning the Dolls House with Doris and Cook

Carol and Peggy

St. Colettes School, Cambridge, 1939

The Wendy House

Garden Tea Party

Barcombe House, Sussex

Langford Grove School, 1946

Carol Gilbert and Joan Hopkins

Chapter Eight
Love In The Air, 1942/3

One summer's day, three boys came into the garden where Carol was playing with Skeet. Their mother was in the consulting room with Dr. Gilbert, her fourth baby due quite soon. Such a beautiful day – how could it possibly have led to so much unhappiness?

The eldest son, John, told Carol that their father was the newly-appointed Squadron Commander at the Bottisham base, and they had been looking at houses in the area to rent, but it seemed as though the baby might arrive before they had found anywhere.

Mrs. Gilbert immediately organised everyone, moving furniture, putting up camp beds, sorting blankets, sheets and pillows, so that the Conways could stay at Beaulieu House for as long as necessary.

Within hours, a fourth boy was born, in the old nursery. He was christened in Bottisham parish church, the doctor standing as godfather, and Carol was so moved by the joyous dignity of the occasion that she painted a watercolour in which every person, from the vicar down to the tiny baby, was depicted as a rabbit.

The Conways found a suitable cottage on the boundary of Swaffham Bulbeck and Commercial End, and the Gilberts helped them to move in. David and Carol often went to spend an hour or two with the Conway boys, while their father examined the baby and his mother. The children would play in the back bedroom in bad weather, or take a football or tennis rackets out onto the big field behind their house.

One day the sun disappeared, and Carol suggested they went indoors.

"We can't go in yet," said John with a frown. "The curtains are still closed in the living room. He hasn't finished examining my mother yet."

She heard the bitterness in his voice and realised that something was very wrong, but he avoided her eyes and she knew he would not explain. She did not understand. They stayed outside under the trees, cold and silent, watching for the curtains to be pulled back.

★ ★ ★

Mrs. Gilbert's great friends, Dulcie and Loughnan Pendred, lived in Swaffham Bulbeck too, in an exciting old house full of staircases and hidden closets. Lough was a wood carver, an artist in the craft of creating beautiful sculptures that graced several churches. He was also the producer of an amateur dramatic society called the Bottisham Players, and the doctor volunteered Carol for a part in their next production called *The Poltergeist*.

She had to play the psychic daughter responsible for all the turmoil. She hated being told where to stand, when to move, and how to say her lines, but when after many rehearsals the curtains finally opened on the first performance on stage at the Bottisham Village College, with all her father's patients (no wonder he called them "bodies") staring up at her, as well as her parents and friends, Carol panicked, froze, stammered and somehow struggled through the evening. The curtains finally closed, and the audience began to applaud – the cast stepped forward, holding hands, and bowed, and it was wonderful. For a plain, nervous child, lacking self-confidence, that sea of friendly faces smiling approval at her was a purification that Carol was to seek over and over again in the future.

★ ★ ★

In September, David returned to Oundle, and Carol started to attend Byron House School in Cambridge. The entire school, teachers and pupils, had been evacuated from Highgate in London, and had taken possession of a rambling old house in Huntingdon Road, that had belonged to the Darwin family. Years later it was demolished to make way for the new monstrosity called Fitzwilliam College, though the Lodge house still stands. Lady Darwin lived in a flat not far from the Backs and, once a week, she invited a few of the pupils for afternoon tea.

Mrs. Gilbert walked Carol up to the bus stop outside Millard's shop that first morning, where she waited for the bus with her new satchel, cloth-covered gas mask, three biscuits in one pocket and an apple in the other. The bus was a single-decker, and during the War, all the seats had been rearranged to make more room, so people sat round the sides facing inwards towards a stifling crush of strap-hanging passengers swaying together as the bus swerved or accelerated, and trod on each other's bunions as it stopped to squeeze in yet more people. A lady insisted that Carol sat on her knee, so she could at least see the passing landscape over the lady's shoulder.

At Drummer Street everyone scrambled out, and Carol headed for the 101 bus to Girton, getting off right outside her new school. She was very proud of her independence.

There were no more than ten pupils in each class, and each subject was taught with enthusiasm by the team of ladies – Mrs. Thornley the Head, Miss Stephens who had been to China and showed the pupils how to write Chinese characters, and Miss Henderson. On warm days, everyone sat on the grass under the big trees in the garden, learning

French, History, Geography and Maths, or they stood by large wooden easels drawing or painting the flowers and people around them. Carol was very shy, and spoke to no-one for several days.

The English teacher asked her class to write a play. Carol's was called *The Bus Queue*, and the teacher read it out to the class. She asked Carol to produce it, and it was a great success when performed in front of the whole school. It was very short – each person in the queue was accosted in turn by an offensive and very drunk tramp. One by one they stalked away in disgust until only the tramp was left. When the bus drew up, he jumped on with ease, as sprightly and sober as a spring lamb.

Carol was "someone" at last. Her reputation as a writer grew when she confessed that Uncle Mac had once accepted a short story of hers, about rabbits.

Her new friends were Anthea Hume and Anne Harris. Carol made a small teddy bear for each of them, as a token of their friendship, and called them Plum, Cherry and Apple. Suddenly Carol seemed to find a lot to talk about, and to her secret delight, her classmates nicknamed her Babble. School was exciting, even the daily hour and a half of homework, and she hardly missed David at all, and only Wisbech now and again.

But then a Relief Bus was introduced to alleviate the crowded early morning crush. It started from the bus stop outside Millard's, so there was plenty of room for the Bottisham people to sit down. Most of the other passengers were village children going to the County School in Cambridge, and they stared at Carol derisively, and nudged each other. A large black-haired girl spoke very loudly:

"Look at 'er! Little miss stuck-up from the big 'ouse! Margarine wouldn't melt in 'er mouth!" She got up, and minced up and down the bus, one hand on hip, saying in a false refined accent:

"Look at me, then – but don't you dare speak to me, you common peasants. I'm much too posh for the likes of you!"

Hot tears stung Carol's eyes, and she wanted to die. Overwhelmed with shame, when more people got in at the Church, she gave up her seat to a lady carrying a baby so she could strap-hang at the front of the bus and stare miserably out of the window, knowing she would have to endure the same ordeal every single day.

With immense courage, Carol prepared herself for the offensive, as she climbed into the bus the following morning. The others were already seated, giggling and pointing. She stood quite still in front of them and gave her tormentor of the previous day a long withering look. After a few seconds, she said, with exaggerated scorn: "Don't be so stupid!" Then she turned on her heel, and strode up the bus as far away from them as possible. Carol opened a book and read all the way to Cambridge, her heart beating like a trapped butterfly.

After that, she ignored them completely, and they gave up trying to bait her. But she was very unhappy inside: why did these young people resent her so? A gulf had appeared between the Gilberts and the villagers that none of them could have anticipated. Even if War made people equal in their shared troubles, why should it have destroyed respect, civility and friendship? The old men of the village still doffed their caps when they met the family in the village shop, but the other customers would mutter angrily when the doctor pushed his way to the head of the queue as he always did, claiming his right to be served first which had been perfectly acceptable in the past, even encouraged by everyone else, who would stand aside with pleasure for their doctor. Things were changing fast.

The Luftwaffe began their "Baedeker" raids, choosing beautiful cities and university towns for their nightly bombing sorties. One bomb fell right outside Carol's school, leaving an enormous crater. Frank Reeve, bookseller of Bowes and Bowes and auxiliary fireman, lived nearby in Woodlark Road, and when the siren sounded he pedalled furiously onto Huntingdon Road where he was overtaken by one of his fire fighting colleagues in his small car. It sped past him and promptly disappeared. He had driven straight into the bomb crater in the dark, from which he emerged somewhat dazed and dishevelled.

Damage to the school was fortunately only minimal, and lessons carried on as normal. Anthea told Carol how the boarders had quietly taken refuge in the alcove under the turn of the stairs as they had often practised with Miss Thornley, but suddenly the windows blew in and they thought the house was about to collapse. There was dust everywhere but amazingly no structural damage.

Several houses in Cambridge had been demolished during that air raid, but happily the magnificent colleges and churches were untouched. On the wall of a bombed-out pub someone drew a Chad – an egg-shaped head with crosses for eyes and a long nose hanging over a wall – with the words "WOT – NO BEER?" Chads appeared in the most unlikely places and cheered everyone up. Posters were stuck on every available space with line drawings by Fougasse and the words "WALLS HAVE EARS" and "CARELESS TALK COSTS LIVES", but gossip still flourished in the Waiting Room, and in the village shops. A sudden silence would descend if a stranger should appear, because Spies were known to be incredibly good at disguising themselves as tramps, onion sellers and even nuns. Yet when Carol went into Pollendine's shop or Bedford's Stores to get Granny's weekly egg, people stopped talking and looked away as if she was a spy! She had no idea why.

Her father often received mysterious phone calls, usually during meal-times, and somehow he seemed to know when one was due, because he would drum his fingers anxiously on the table. He always took those calls in his surgery, and minutes later he would put on his coat, saying:

"I have to go out – I have been called to a Meeting." Carol soon realised that the Meeting was with Mrs. Conway, and hoped her mother did not know. She did of course. Equally she must have prayed that her children were unaware of what was going on.

To give him some credit, the doctor did try to salve his conscience during this difficult time by taking Carol to the theatre, to concerts, art exhibitions and encouraging her to paint and draw. So she heard Dame Myra Hess playing the piano at the Guildhall midday concerts, and later Paderewski, and Rawicz and Landauer.

He took Carol to the Arts Theatre to see *Pagliacci* and *The Barber of Seville* but most wonderfully let her see the great American actress Ruth Draper, who portrayed dozens of characters, often several at a time, yet entirely alone on the stage. In one scene she played the part of a frightened Russian immigrant sitting on her suitcase at New York docks, surrounded by strangers milling around her. Some years later Carol saw Joyce Grenfell creating much the same magic, and her desire to emulate both of them led her eventually to Drama School.

The doctor and Carol shared a joyful delight in these excursions and became very close. Sometimes David accompanied them when he was at home from boarding school, but their mother never came. Her relationship with her husband had become difficult, although she never changed in her attitude to him. But no matter what she said or did, he found fault, picking on her suggestions, her comments, her clothes, and her ability to manage the household.

David would rise to her defence immediately, so Carol instinctively supported her father. David and Carol always disagreed with each other anyway, as a matter of principle, but he became aggressive and morose, shutting himself away in his room, and shutting her out from his misery which must have equalled her own.

With their parents so preoccupied with avoiding each other, it is perhaps not surprising that neither of them thought to explain fully to Carol the Facts of Life. David had confided to her some years before that babies were started in the vestry during the wedding ceremony, and she knew how Mrs. Perkins became pregnant three times a year thanks to a raucous band of tom cats. But when she found blood in her knickers accompanied by a dreadful pain, she thought she was dying of some dreadful disease. Granny found her crouching on the staircase, consoled her with great tenderness, and told her all about the Curse. Her father just gave her some pain-killers.

Carol refused to appear in the garden in her knitted swimsuit because her chest was bulging out at the sides, so her mother took her to Eaden Lilleys and bought her a "bust bodice", also a proper swimming costume, some sanitary towels and a special belt. She was only eleven, but she was to learn about sex very soon.

One of their RAF boys, Roger, was a particular friend of the cabaret singer Frances Day who was about to visit Cambridge to entertain the troops in the area. He asked if Frances could come and spend the weekend at Beaulieu House. Greatly excited, Mrs. Gilbert and Carol prepared David's room for her, and she duly arrived in a bright red sports car, wearing a fantastic fur coat, and the whole of the back of the car was filled with primroses. When Carol came home from school that day, the entire Squadron seemed to be crammed into David's room upstairs. She tried to peer through the jostling blue uniforms, when a deep rich voice said:

"All right, boys, that's enough! You're keeping my public away. Let the little girl through."

They stood aside, and she smiled directly at Carol. Tall, elegant, her hair loose around her bare shoulders, she seemed to have been poured into the close-fitting satin dress. She was beautiful. She sent all the boys away, except Roger, and motioned Carol to stay while she got ready to give an impromptu concert downstairs.

"I'm going to do my legs, darling. Can't get silk stockings these days."

She sat on the bed, pulled up the dress to her waist, and began to colour her legs using a brown liquid poured onto cotton wool. She started at her feet, and worked slowly upwards. Carol could not take her eyes off her. Neither could Roger.

When she was satisfied that both legs were equally brown, she said, "Now we come to the tricky bit. Roger is going to draw the seams in for me." She paused, and then added "Perhaps you had better run along now, darling." She beckoned Carol closer and whispered, "Roger is rather shy."

It was some time later that Frances Day made a magnificent entrance into the drawing room, and everyone cheered and clapped. Her pianist opened the piano, and she sang several melodies, with inevitably, "De-lovely, de-lightful, de-lectable, de-licious" – and so she was.

She spent most of the weekend quietly resting, the glamour put away in the wardrobe. Carol thought she was the most wonderful person in the world, and vowed to become a star like her one day.

She told her friends at school all about Frances Day and the painted stockings, and they were scandalized. They tried colouring their legs with brown powder paint but it dried into a blotchy mess, and brown crayon was quite useless for drawing seams because it tickled and they could not get the lines straight. Roger must have had plenty of practice.

Shortly after meeting the adorable Frances Day, Carol fell hopelessly in love with Henry Joy. He was in his early twenties and the day he arrived at the house she showed him upstairs to the little room that was to be his, overlooking the garden, and helped him to unpack his kitbag. He put a photograph on his dressing table.

"That's my wife, and that's my little girl. I'm going to miss her a lot. Will you be my little girl from now on, Carol?" His bright blue eyes smiled into hers, and she was enraptured.

"Yes, I will," she promised.

Carol became his slave, his confidante, and his batman, polishing the buttons on his uniform, mending his socks, even ironing his shirts. She could hardly wait to get home from school each day, to put fresh flowers in his room. Whenever he was flying with the squadron into action, she would creep into his room and hug Cordy, his little corduroy dog mascot, and prayed to God to keep a special eye on the RAF.

Inevitably the awful day came when Henry was posted elsewhere, and Carol thought her heart would break. He gave her a little china dog as a leaving present.

"He is called Roy, of course – Cordy's Roy". He said, as he hugged her goodbye.

Carol was disconsolate, crying at the slightest thing, and her father suggested that her mother took her to Oundle to see David one weekend. (No doubt he would arrange to be pleasantly occupied during their absence.)

They stayed at the Talbot Hotel where Carol borrowed a Scottie called Angel Pavement from another guest, and introduced him to the cows in a nearby meadow.

David showed them round the school, introduced them to the Headmaster, Mr. Fisher, whose son James was a great friend of Mrs. Gilbert's brother Eric Ennion, both highly acclaimed ornithologists. Then Carol spotted a tubby little man hurrying across the courtyard.

"That's Arthur Marshall," muttered David, "my art teacher. You know him as 'Nurse Dugdale' from the radio." Mr. Marshall seemed far too short and ordinary to be the man behind the comic lady's voice, as Carol was quite sure that Nurse Dugdale was very tall, and built like a battleship to match her foghorn voice.

They joined the whole school for the Sunday morning service in the Chapel, sitting at the back with other parents, and marvelling as the boys' voices filled the vaulted roof. Then Mr. Fisher read out a list of past pupils recently killed in action, whose names would soon join the many others inscribed on the In Memoriam panels behind them.

On the way home in the train, her mother asked Carol what she thought of boarding schools. Carol shrugged.

"Oh, all right, I suppose."

"Daddy is going to write to one or two excellent schools that we have heard about, and we can talk it over when they send us the Prospectuses."

Carol had never considered the idea of being sent away from home all by herself, but several of her friends at Byron House were boarders and seemed quite happy.

She cycled over to see Nursie in her Little Haven in Lode, close to Anglesey Abbey, and watched shyly as she breastfed her new baby and then changed his nappy, but she did not feel able to tell Nursie her problems as she had done in the past.

★ ★ ★

With David away, Nursie busy with her own family, Henry gone probably forever, Carol felt very lonely. She was also acutely aware that the relationship between her parents was in danger of collapsing although they both tried very hard to behave "normally" in her presence. Carol decided to run away.

She would have to take Skeet and Mrs. Perkins with her, of course, which would be difficult, and while she planned this adventure, she drew a large picture of the three of them in some distant part of the country, with her bike and a hold-all, looking up at a signpost pointing to Scotland one way and Wales the other. It took a long time to draw and then she painted it with watercolours, so by the time it was finished, her desire to run away had completely gone.

Chapter Nine
Yankee Doodles, 1943/4

Carol made a new friend at school – Anna Jooss. Her family had escaped from Germany and they were living in the converted roof space over Dr. Roughton's garage near Grange Road. Kurt Jooss was rebuilding his ballet company in England, helped by his musical director Leder, and they had produced new, exciting and controversial ballets in a free, expressive style quite unlike the stiff, classical poses of the Sadler Wells and other companies Carol had seen with their irritating bouncing cygnets. This was a marriage of music and passion that made her nerves tingle when her father took her to see them at the Arts Theatre, performing *The Green Room* and *Spectre de la Rose*.

Anna invited Carol round to meet her parents. Mrs. Jooss was very frail and spoke no English: Kurt was quite short and solid, a most untypical ballet dancer, with wispy brown hair fluffing out on either side of a completely bald patch on top of his head, rather like a garden gnome.

He suggested that Carol might like to join one of the company's ballet classes, which he held in the big drawing room of Dr. Roughton's house with all the carpets rolled up out of the way. Fortunately, Anna came too or Carol would not have stayed, not knowing what was expected of her.

After some warming up exercises, they sat still on the floor and listened to a gramophone record. The music began wistfully, and then arched into a sad crescendo. Kurt began to sway to the music, and one by one the others rose and allowed their whole bodies to respond, each in their own way, each performing their own private dance. For Kurt, Tchaikovsky was torment, fear, rebellion, ecstasy. He expressed the terrors that had befallen his own family and friends, and it was wonderful, terrifying, to watch.

Carol stood up and began to dance, too, as the music commanded, flowing into her and out through her fingertips, her arms, her feet. When the music stopped, they were exhausted but triumphant.

"Beautiful, my darlings," said Kurt. "Now you know what dancing really means!"

★ ★ ★

During the summer of 1943, the RAF began to pack up and leave Bottisham. Apparently the US Army Air Force was due to occupy the camp quite soon.

Carol hated to see Poundie go, and her mother cried too. He had become her special friend and confidant. A few weeks later they heard that he had married the widow of an old friend. Soon Bottisham was deserted, the villagers bereft and aimless, silent as they waited in the queues for their rations.

Mrs. Conway and her four boys moved into a mill house near Quy, apparently for the "duration", so that the older boys could stay at the local school, while her husband was transferred elsewhere. Besides, there was soon to be a fifth baby.

Carol was walking home from Bedford's shop one morning with Granny's ration of one egg and a small pat of butter, when an army vehicle hurtled towards her on the wrong side of the road. The driver stopped, and grinned at her.

"Hi ya, Red!" he called, and threw something at her before the jeep roared away. It was an orange – she could remember oranges from before the War, but this was the first one that she had actually held in her hands for nearly six years.

Carol found her mother drooling over a large cardboard box in the kitchen, pulling out tins of meat, biscuits, more fruit and – oh, wondrous sight! - bars of chocolate.

"The Yanks have arrived!" she explained. "The new Commander, Colonel Christian, just brought these for us. Isn't it marvellous?"

Later that afternoon, a great convoy of troops rumbled into the village, the soldiers tossing oranges, chocolates and chewing gum down to the excited children who clamoured after them.

★ ★ ★

The first billeted American to stay at Beaulieu House was a big, broad Major from Texas, Roy Webb, and he too called Carol "Red". He brought her a box of candies, a doll with clothes and a little teddy bear. Captain Weldon T. Ross came next, equally laden with gifts. Every day seemed to be Christmas.

They were the kindest of men, generous and warm, and always immensely polite. Carol offered to shine their shoes, but they were not too concerned about their appearance, lounging about with open-necked shirts and even going to camp in crumpled uniforms. They never seemed to be in a hurry either. They loved to sprawl in deckchairs in the garden after dinner with fat brown cigars between their teeth, and talk about life and the "folks back home".

At breakfast they consumed bacon, eggs, toast and marmalade all on one large plate, washed down with mugs of coffee. All this was courtesy of the USAAF stores of course – the family's meagre rations appalled their guests and so they were showered with whatever they needed.

★ ★ ★

Skeet and Carol met Ursula in the park by the lake one day, and she introduced Carol to her "Marmy" at the old gardener's cottage into which they had recently moved. Her father was an "arficer". They had peanut butter and strawberry jam sandwiches to which Carol was immediately addicted.

The village children chewed gum interminably, said "gee" and "shucks", and sported T-shirts presented by the GIs from the huge American air base at Mildenhall. The girls wore nylon stockings, eminently better than bare, brown-stained legs, and every Saturday night dances were held in the Lecture Hall. Coach loads of "chicks" were brought from Cambridge, much to the annoyance of the local girls. The sounds of revelry would keep Carol awake, and she would lean out of her bedroom window, catch sight of moving figures among the rose beds, and shout, "I can see you!"

Inevitably her father became very busy as the birth rate increased dramatically, and consequently the vicar solemnised innumerable Anglo-American marriages.

★ ★ ★

Every Thursday evening, Joan Russell and Carol helped their mothers to cut sandwiches and wash-up at the camp canteen. It was deafeningly noisy, and Carol's hands ached with opening bottle after bottle of Coca-Cola. The Yanks had decorated the canteen walls with lewd pictures of near-naked ladies, and even painted lipstick on the cups. The GIs all teased her and called her "Red", but in the most respectful way.

The Gilberts were invited by the Colonel to see a film in the lecture hall about resistance fighters in occupied France, but they had to leave when the film ended, walking past rows of cat-calling GIs, and once the family had gone, they were apparently shown highly secret films, plans and diagrams of imminent operational raids.

The local boys played cricket with the Americans, who in turn taught them how to play baseball. Ursula came to Byron House with Carol, and they travelled together on the bus, united in their disdain of the County School kids.

Part of the field opposite Beaulieu House was now required to house the growing numbers of GIs, and long accommodation blocks and Nissen huts were soon erected. Colonel Christian escorted the Gilberts around the site. Here was to be a new hospital, fully equipped with several wards, an operating theatre, dental laboratory, and its own catering facilities. He asked the doctor to act as a special medical advisor to the station, and Dick was immensely proud to accept.

Colonel Christian was a charming man, and because he insisted on flying on missions with his men, he took the same risk that they all did, and one day he failed to return. His plane had been shot down. The family were bereft and mourned him as a member of their own family.

★ ★ ★

Christmas 1943 was unforgettable. Their American friends dug up a fir tree from somewhere, and smothered it with coloured lights and tinsel. It stood in the hall near the stairs, and grew dozens of parcels over night. Major Webb dressed up as Santa Claus and handed presents to everyone. They even had a traditional Christmas Dinner, thanks to the USAAF.

In the afternoon, the Ennion cousins came over from Burwell, and the children played hide and seek, and drawing games at which Uncle Eric excelled. Then they gathered round the piano and sang carols.

Dr. Gilbert had put up a huge map of Europe on the living room wall, and pinned a piece of red wool across the toe of Italy where the Allies were beginning an offensive. From the first week of 1944, that red line moved steadily north. As spring came, there was increasing activity in the camp, and the Major said that he was going on embarkation leave, and that soon the entire group would be leaving, presumably going abroad. The build-up for D-Day had begun.

The Major took photos of the family, the house and the garden, and wrote in Carol's autograph book: "Remember when it's all over that I'll value and remember the friendship of the Gilberts".

The entire village went into mourning with the departure of the Americans. Their warmth and generosity had touched all their lives and they would never be forgotten.

On 6 June 1944, the Allies landed on the beaches of France, and the little, red, wool line began to creep towards Germany. However, Hitler had a final surprise: Flying Bombs, better known as Doodlebugs. They passed overhead like little finned bombs with fire in their tails, until the flames suddenly stopped, and there was an eerie silence. That was the time to take cover. The bombs slowed, turned towards earth, and crashed with an enormous explosion. Many of them were shot down by anti-aircraft guns as they crossed the Channel, but too many got through and caused terrible damage and loss of life. But still Bottisham remained unscathed.

★ ★ ★

Dr. Gilbert was introduced to a couple staying in Cambridge, Mr. and Mrs. Barry Craig, and he told his family with great excitement that this "chappie" was a professional painter who had exhibited at the Royal Academy, so he had invited them for the weekend and had even commissioned this "chappie" to do a portrait.

Mrs. Gilbert was thrilled.

"Which of the children will he be painting, or perhaps both of them together?"

The doctor frowned. "Of course not. Neither of them."

"Surely not me?" exclaimed his wife.

"Certainly not," he retorted. "He will be painting a portrait of me, of course."

So Barry came, and the commission was agreed. He and his wife came to the house two or three times a week, until the portrait was finished. The doctor was seated on a chair with an Indian carpet nailed on the wall behind him, and Mrs. Craig played Brahms while Barry painted, talking quietly about his daughter, Ming. She was a boarder at an unusual school, Langford Grove, now evacuated from Sussex to Herefordshire. It was run by an eccentric ex-opera singer who encouraged barefoot dancing on the lawn, and piano practice all day long in preference to mundane lessons. Even more appealing to the doctor was the claim that, "Anyone who was somebody in literary and artistic society sent their daughters to Langford Grove", so it was obviously just the place for Carol. Her father wrote a letter to Mrs. Curtis asking her to accept his daughter as a boarder the following year, in spring 1945.

★ ★ ★

A small contingent of Belgian airmen took over the camp, and marched proudly through the village in their blue uniforms. Two officers were billeted with the Gilberts: Georges, who was also a doctor, brought with him his beautiful young wife, Georgette, and Pierre. He had an incredibly sad face, preferring to stay in his room rather than make small-talk with the rest of the household.

Mrs. Gilbert eventually told Carol that Pierre had escaped when the Germans invaded Belgium, but for some reason his wife stayed behind. She worked for the

Resistance, blowing up bridges and railway lines and
generally making life awkward for the Germans. But she
was caught and eventually died in a concentration camp.
Meanwhile Pierre managed to reach England and joined the
large number of expatriates fighting alongside the British
troops. It was a long time before he found out what had
happened to his wife, and he blamed himself for not forcing
her to leave when he did.

A young friend of Georges at the camp was a brilliant
piano player, but there was no instrument in his billet. He
was invited to come and play whenever he wished. So
Hubert Casin called one evening with a few friends and
played for them – Schubert, Brahms, Chopin, a medley of
Vera Lynn songs, and the latest American dance rhythm
which he called the Jitterbug. Hubert's friend insisted on
demonstrating this incredible dance, using Carol like a sack
of potatoes, whirling her round, down through his legs and
up into the air. He introduced himself as Albert, Prince de
Ligne, owner of a small island in the middle of a huge river
in the Belgian Congo. He was so handsome that Carol
believed every word he said. But it was all true.

After that, Hubert called nearly every day, tiptoeing into
the drawing room so as not to disturb Mrs. Gilbert dusting
the bedrooms, but she would listen enraptured to the
melodies of Ivor Novello or Irving Berlin, or a Beethoven
prelude, swirling up the stairs. Sometimes he played sad,
tortured music, so everyone kept away, knowing he was
thinking of Belgium. But he would soon crash into a frenzy
of jazz.

He was not at all handsome, in fact quite ugly in a
delightful way, and the girls adored him. He would go to
the Tea Dances at the Dorothy Café in Cambridge, and
literally sweep them off their feet.

Once a week, or so it seemed, Hubert would bring his
latest girlfriend to meet the Gilberts, and anxiously ask Mrs.

Gilbert for her approval. He desperately wanted to get married, but needed a second opinion before popping the question. Mrs. Gilbert tried to give a fair judgement.

Then one day he brought home a dark, attractive girl and exclaimed:

"Voilà! This is the one! See? We are married this morning!"

Only weeks later came the wonderful news that the Allies had liberated Belgium. But Hubert never knew. He was killed just a few days before, when his plane was shot down during a raid over Germany. It was a terrible waste of such unique talent, and such a beloved friend.

Their Belgian guests came to toast "La Belgique libre" with the family, and they all stood around the silent piano with tears streaming down their faces.

Sorrow never comes singly. One morning Skeet did not get up from his bed in the kitchen. The vet came while Carol was out in the garden and she heard the car crunching on the gravel drive. She waited and prayed until the car left, and then her father came out to find her. She knew the old dog was dead.

They gave him a magnificent funeral. He was wrapped in blankets and the doctor carried him into the air-raid shelter. Not once in the past few years had it been used for its intended purpose, so perhaps Wisbech had unknowingly dug it for this special and eternal purpose. The bunks and Carol's paintings had long since been removed, so her father covered the base with soil, laid the dog inside and solemnly filled the whole shelter with earth before sealing it from the outside world.

Soon it would be spring, and daffodils would grow on the little mound.

Chapter Ten
Upper-Crust Boarders, 1945

O n 6 May 1945, Carol and her mother travelled by train to Hereford, and a taxi deposited them and Carol's trunk at the Kings Arms in Kington, the nearest small town to the wartime home of Langford Grove School for Girls.

Carol slept badly, conscious of the hills crowding the view, missing the flat Fenlands and wide skies. The hotel was humming with the news that the end of the War was imminent, with arrangements being made for the Germans to surrender the following day. Mrs. Gilbert phoned the school, and was advised not to arrive until the ninth, so they spent the day walking the hills and talking about the past seven momentous years, the events and the people that had changed "the even tenure" of their lives. But neither of them mentioned the Conways.

The next morning crowds gathered in the little town. Flags and bunting were looped from every upstairs window to the one opposite, and a rope had been slung across the main street pegged out with vests, long johns, stockings, shirts and knickers, with "The Siegfried Line" scrawled in ink across a sheet. People in uniform, mothers and children, stood quietly waiting for the broadcast at ten o'clock which was relayed from the hotel wireless turned up as loud as possible.

"The War is over!" and everyone cheered, cried, shouted, clapped, hugged each other and danced the conga in and out of the crowds. Above the clamour they heard the sound that many old people had feared never to hear again – the joyous ringing of church bells. Silent for seven years, ready to announce the dreaded invasion of Britain that never materialised, they now sang of liberation throughout the country.

The party continued all day and all night, and there were still weary revellers staggering through the debris when Mrs. Gilbert and Carol left Kington in a taxi, heading for Eywood near Titley.

Years later, when Carol read Daphne du Maurier's *Rebecca* and the description of the new Mrs. De Winter arriving at Manderley, she could see Eywood at once: a big sprawling house at the end of a long, fern-lined drive, with the figure of a woman standing menacingly on the top step in front of an enormous front door. Not Mrs. Danvers – this was Matron.

She looked stern, forbidding, ramrod straight, but she was smiling.

"Yew must be Carol," she said. (A Scottish Matron.) "No-one else has arrived yet. They'll be coming on the train tomorrow, nae doot."

The taxi-driver deposited the trunk in the hall and agreed to wait ten minutes while Mrs. Gilbert settled Carol in.

Matron led them up a wide staircase to the dormitories, and showed Carol the one that she was to share with eleven other girls. Then she took them downstairs again to see the dining room, the library, several classrooms, and the kitchen. This was the only room in the whole house that did not have its own piano.

Carol hugged her mother, trying not to cry, and then she was gone. Carol watched her hand waving from the taxi until it was out of sight, and began to unpack her trunk. Each bed had its own chest of drawers, and there was a row of wardrobes at one end of the room. Carol found a bathroom along the corridor nearly as big as the dormitory, empty but for one huge stained bath with iron claw feet. Another room had been converted to enclose three toilet cubicles.

Matron and Carol shared a cheese sandwich in the kitchen, and discussed the victory in Europe.

"Aye, there's still a lot of fighting going on in the Pacific," she sighed. "But at least the Jerries are beaten!"

The next morning Carol watched the girls arrive in small groups, shouting greetings to their friends and grabbing the best beds. She crept away and explored the garden – there was an enormous lake with a boathouse, encircled by over-grown rhododendron bushes, rose beds, walled gardens, and an orangery which proved to be a good hiding place. All around the house and garden was dense woodland, with here and there worn pathways that led to a rabbit warren, or perhaps a fox's lair. She also discovered tennis courts, a stable yard and a vegetable garden.

Matron was supervising the unpacking, and insisted that the girls take their term's supply of sanitary towels to a vast cupboard on the landing. From there she would hand them out as requested, but they were invariably of inferior quality to those the girls had brought, and they never knew who received the nice soft expensive ones.

That evening Mrs. Curtis arrived, and they were all summoned to her sitting room. She was formidable – tall, with thick golden hair plaited on top of her head, and topped by a large straw hat trailing ribbons. Her dress seemed to float around her and was tied comfortably around her waist by a long scarf. Her pale-green eyes were larger than normal, almost bulging.

"Because she cried so much when her husband died," Carol was informed.

She welcomed them to Langford Grove in a high, clear, carefully articulated voice. She was undeniably eccentric but it was all part of her great charm. She always wore a hat and trailing scarves indoors as well as out, and her chief mission in running the private school was to encourage talented girls to receive the very best instruction in music and art, even at the expense of more academic learning.

That night Carol suddenly felt terribly alone and miserable, and she began to cry. Her sobs were heard by Sally Prince, who crept over to her bed and put her arms around her.

"Don't cry, dear – you will feel homesick at first; we all do. But if you cry out loud you will upset everyone else. We are all being brave and hiding our feelings."

★ ★ ★

Carol soon learnt that Curty (the girls' name for Mrs. Curtis) regularly liked to send for them after they had gone to bed, to come and listen to concerts on the wireless with her, sitting on little wooden chairs or cushions on the floor of her spacious sitting room. When the studio audience began to clap at the end of each piece, Curty would turn off the sound. She hated to hear applause, despite her years as an opera singer.

Mrs. Curtis often invited friends to stay at Langford Grove, many of them parents of her "gels", and they were expected to give their criticism of the school work according to their own particular talents. So Ben Nicholson and Rowland Hilder had to look at their paintings – and one day Frances Hodgkins peered over Carol's shoulder and sighed deeply at her farmyard drawings. Musical parents endured endless renderings of Bach fugues and Chopin études.

J.B. Priestley arrived for a weekend, to see his daughter Rachel. Long after the girls had gone to bed, Matron marched into the dormitory calling:

"Wake up! Mrs. Curtis wants you all downstairs for *Comic Cuts!*"

They dressed quickly, clattered downstairs and found Curty ensconced in her velvet chair with J.B. Priestley seated on the other side of the fireplace. She asked them to perform *Pride and Predjudice*. Carol had never read the book.

A huge wooden box was dragged into the middle of the carpet, and they grabbed the clothes inside – hooped skirts, shawls, gloves, top hats, bonnets – while a self-selected producer gave them a quick run-down of the story and told them which character each one was to play. A sofa was placed at an angle in front of the window, "Mrs. Bennett" sat down regally, fluttering her fan, and the impromptu play began.

It lasted only about ten minutes even though they managed to incorporate every nuance of the book, and they were duly congratulated and sent back to bed. Fortunately command performances of *Comic Cuts* only occurred once or twice a term, but it was a daunting experience for a new boarder.

★ ★ ★

Another of Curty's visitors was an ancient American lady, festooned with wrinkles and jewellery, called Madeleine Z. Doty. She had been a suffragette alongside Mrs. Pankhurst and her daughters, and had stayed many times with the Pethick Laurences in London. The girls sat on the floor in the drawing room listening enraptured to her reminiscences, of being chained to railings, shouting at policemen, and going on hunger strike in prison. Mrs. Curtis felt no doubt, and quite rightly, that her "gels" would learn far more from such personal anecdotes than they would from a history teacher.

Curty's policy on education was clear – all her pupils belonged to financially secure, socially acceptable families, so they would not anticipate having to earn a living. Subjects such as mathematics, geography and scripture were regarded as inferior to English and history, with music, drama and art of the utmost importance.

On fine mornings all the girls were sent out onto the lawn to dance to the music of Elgar, bare footed devotees of Isadora Duncan, the wind-up gramophone balanced precariously on the balustrade. Art classes were held in what had once been the stables, each girl creating a masterpiece of still life or imaginary nightmares on huge easels with oils or watercolours, while the weedy voice of John McCormack bleated about his Vienna from that same gramophone now in the middle of the room.

There were timetables pinned up everywhere, not just for lessons but for piano practice which was far more important. Every piano in every room in the house was in constant use and the standard of the players was incredibly high. Carol could not compete so did not try.

There had to be something else that she could do which would at least give her confidence, if not recognition, and provide some justification for her attendance at this highly creative institution.

At Eywood, there were only two or three professional teachers who shared all the classes between them. One was a refugee from Austria, who taught French and needlework. Her entire wardrobe was hand-knitted in off-white wool – skirts, jackets, dresses, even her stockings. She also wept copiously while demonstrating the blanket stitch, but became ecstatic when Helen Mann and Carol asked if she would teach them German. It was a suspicious request at a time when anything German was still regarded as evil, even dachshund dogs. But their parents agreed and they learnt the new language together at remarkable speed.

Later, Carol was to stay with Helen during the summer holiday, in Winston Churchill's constituency at Woodford, Essex. The house seemed full of children, pianos and cellos, with instrumentalists popping in to form a trio or a quartet at various times of the day. Helen's eldest brother, Bo, was a music critic for *The Times*, although he was still an undergraduate at Cambridge. Mrs. Mann cooked huge meals for this extended family, and Carol was very impressed that she always added a glass of wine to the gravy and a glass of sherry to the custard.

★ ★ ★

The most exciting event of that first term was the arrival of the actors. The first troupe was composed entirely of masculine women with short haircuts and baggy trousers, who performed an abridged Shakespeare play, sharing two-dozen parts between them. The girls found the love scenes particularly distasteful, especially as Shakespeare had written his plays for male actors only, giving some of his lines a special irony which was entirely lost by this performance. Their mobile home had once been a char-à-banc, and it housed all their possessions, costumes, scenery, and props, as well as cooking equipment and bedding.

The other theatrical company were all French, four girls and two extremely handsome young men. They performed a short play by Molière, and an intriguing piece in mime. Curty insisted that "les jolies filles" should sleep in the sickbay over the stables, while the boys put up a tent on the grass near the lake.

Carol was woken sharply in the early hours of the morning by the scrape of the window beside her bed being pushed up. Sarah stepped into the room, her nightie soaking wet, followed by a very damp, inebriated Julia. They giggled as they stumbled into their beds, and Carol pretended she had not seen them. The next morning, Curty summoned all the girls into the library.

"Last night a figure was spotted climbing up a drainpipe near one of the dormitories," she declared, "according to Fräulein Schmidt, who happened to look out of a window on her way to the… hm, bathroom. Well? Who was it?" She glowered at each pupil in turn.

They all looked blankly at each other and no-one owned up. They knew that the French group had already packed up and left even before breakfast, so could not be questioned.

Later in the privacy of their classroom, Sarah and Julia described their adventure, to their friends' immense admiration and envy – the tryst with the two boys by the lake at midnight, the bottle of wine and the French cigarettes shared between them, then the chasing games around the bushes and the quick embrace, before the exhilarating swim across the lake.

Someone betrayed their confidence however, and Sarah and Julia were sent home. Of course, being expelled from Langford Grove was an achievement, not a disgrace. It showed initiative and character.

★ ★ ★

Towards the end of term, the girls performed *The Reluctant Dragon* by Lady Gregory, after five or six fraught rehearsals, before a critical audience of girls, staff and Mrs. Curtis.

No-one had actually learned their lines so they read them from heavily marked French's Acting Editions as they blundered about among the chairs and tables carefully set out on the "stage" area beneath the stairwell in the entrance hall. Carol played the part of the Queen, who did little but stand very straight and bawl at her husband "Al-fred!"

To her amazement every time she yelled "Al-fred!" the audience roared with laughter, and it was a delicious experience. Carol overplayed the character shamelessly, unconsciously basing it on Mrs. Curtis herself, who could be heard every morning standing on the landing outside her private rooms calling "Ma-Tron!"

Carol's popularity soared. She tried to mimic the teachers with surprising success, and realised that she had found her artistic flair and that her future was secure: she was going to be an actress.

★ ★ ★

A large coach collected everyone from Eywood at the end of term, and took them to Hereford for the steam train to Paddington. Somehow Carol struggled across London with her luggage and caught a train from Kings Cross to Cambridge. The pupils each had a letter for their parents from Curty, written in her spidery scrawl, with a brief report on their progress and the advice that during the summer holidays the entire school would be transferring to Sussex, and in September the older girls would be going to Barcombe Mills, while the younger ones, including Carol, would be going to a smaller house at Newick a few miles away. The school's enforced wartime exile from the hub of Culture was over.

Chapter Eleven
Atomic Rebel

C arol arrived home in the middle of Election fever. The
Labour party had left the National Government after
V.E. Day and was now preparing to topple the
Conservatives and the best-loved Prime Minister of all
time, Sir Winston Churchill. Carol was staggered to hear
her father's views: "Churchill brought us through the War,
with his oratory and his dignity, but now we need
something else, new homes for the poor, and all future
wealth to be shared among everyone, rich and poor alike."

Could this be her snobbish father, owner of a large
country house with tennis court and swimming pool,
offering to share all this with the common villagers?

"Just imagine," he sighed, "hospital beds, prescriptions,
all welfare services, dentistry, baby care – all free to
everyone, whatever their class or position in society. A
Labour government would bring in State Medicine, and
that has convinced me above all else."

There were local elections too, for the Parish Council, so
the doctor stood as Labour candidate for Bottisham. Out of
sheer devilment, the village postmaster put himself up as a
Conservative, and won a resounding victory against the
national trend. The doctor was bitterly upset. He had
naturally expected all his patients to vote for him, had
indeed bombarded them in his surgery and on his rounds
with demands that they should do so, but the incongruity of
the situation was not lost on them.

Mrs. Millard in the sweet-shop explained the attitude of the village to Carol: "The Doctor is liked well enough, but as a doctor, not as our representative on the Council. That's the trouble with his party as we see it, dear – there are Labour supporters, and there are Socialists. Your father is hardly working-class like the rest of us, so he must be a socialist."

The dream of a National Health Service was not immediately acceptable to all doctors. Eric Ennion was horrified at "the bogey of State medicine", having to toe the line and write out endless certificates. Fortunately he became involved with the new Field Studies Council, and was offered the tenancy of Flatford Mill, newly owned by the National Trust, and the family moved to East Bergholt that summer of 1945, where Dr. Ennion became the Warden of the first Field Centre. Their windows looked out over the pond in front of Willy Lott's cottage.

★ ★ ★

The camp site beside Beaulieu House was abandoned now, and the Air Ministry allowed the smaller site opposite to become a temporary home for Polish schoolboys and their teachers. The doctor spent many hours talking to them in their own language, asking about their experiences and winning their confidence. He still never spoke to anyone about his early life in Poland, but he was obviously upset by the stories of brutality that the boys told him.

Then an unimagined miracle happened – a letter came from the British Embassy in Paris, to say that Mr. and Mrs. Georges Lwowski were trying to locate Mrs. Lwowski's brother, who was believed to be known as Dr. A.F. Gilbert of Bottisham, near Cambridge. Dick contacted the Ambassador at once, and arranged to go over to Paris where he would hope to make arrangements to bring his sister Gita and her family back to live with him. Gita had always been his favourite sister, the one that Carol most resembled, and his joy at finding that she of all his family, with her husband and little daughter Lulu, had escaped from occupied Poland, thanks almost certainly to a string of Resistance fighters, was surely overwhelming.

He managed to get two seats on one of the few planes accepting passengers, and took David with him to Paris. Brother and sister had so much to say, yet found no words capable of expressing their shared loss; and there were so many tears to wash away the pain before preparing for a new life in a new country together.

It was several months before Gita, Georges and Lulu arrived at Beaulieu House; they spoke not a word of English, so the doctor had to act as interpreter between his wife and his sister. Gita cried almost all the time, crushing Carol to her bosom and stroking her hair. She constantly expressed her love and gratitude to Dick, which clearly embarrassed him so much that he shut himself away in his consulting room whenever she came downstairs from the old nursery that had been converted into a bed/sitting room for them.

He had no time for poor Georges either, who sat in awkward silence with his little girl on his knee, and Carol noticed the leathery hands covered with old cuts and his broken finger nails.

"That's because he worked as a labourer for years," commented her father, and then she understood. Her father was ashamed that his sister had married this working-class man; it was an affront to his personal aspiration to be accepted as a member of respectable middle class society.

The atmosphere at home was becoming more and more chilly. The doctor and his wife spoke to each other only when it was necessary, Dick avoided Georges, and Gita kept on crying. In desperation, the doctor contacted a mill in

Yorkshire, where several displaced Polish people had found refuge, and Georges was offered a job there.

So Georges, Gita and little Lulu left Bottisham and the brief reconciliation was over. They were never to meet again. In 1949 the Lwowski's went to start a new life in Israel, and for several years Gita sent postcards with news of Lulu, but no-one replied.

★ ★ ★

During that long summer holiday, Mrs. Gilbert loved having her children back home, and they invited school friends to stay – David's friends slept in the attic rooms, and the girls took breakfast up to them much earlier than necessary.

They played tennis, table tennis, and swam while Carol watched, and in the evenings they moved the furniture in the living room, rolled up the carpet, and danced to 78 records of Victor Sylvester and Joe Loss.

★ ★ ★

The doctor was busy visiting his patients as usual, but he avoided going to see "that woman" as David called her. Carol had guessed that David was aware of the liaison, and though they never mentioned it, she knew she could talk to him if she ever needed to.

The doctor now spent hours in his Dark Room, which had once been the small front bedroom where Carol had worshipped Henry. Here he practised his new hobby, developing negatives, enlarging prints and washing them in watery trays under an orange gloom. He became a keen photographer, posing a reluctant David and Carol in various corners of the garden, or indoors with all the lights on and an anglepoise lamp placed precariously on a chair, blinding the sitter while Dick fussed over his tripod and his camera to achieve the best possible effect.

Then on 6 August, the atom bomb was dropped on Hiroshima, and days later America destroyed Nagasaki too with unimaginable consequences. The family saw the devastating effect of the atomic bombs on the cinema screen the following week.

★ ★ ★

At the beginning of September, Mrs. Gilbert travelled with Carol as far as Victoria Station, from where she and her school friends took a train to Lewes in Sussex. There they were met by a private coach that took them to the village of Newick. Curty and Matron were already with the senior girls at Barcombe Mills, so the junior girls were under the supervision of Nurse MacLaren and the housekeeper, Miss Kettle.

There were only a dozen girls, so little or no trouble was expected.

They were wrong, of course.

There were two dormitories, six beds in each one, and that first night they began whispering to each other after lights out, about holidays, pets, and Hiroshima.

"At least the Japs have surrendered."

"Yes, but the Americans have got the atomic bomb and they could use it again if they wanted to – and there is nothing that can stop them."

"One might go off by mistake."

"Oh, shut up!"

"But it might! Say one was dropped by mistake on London – you know what damage it would do. How would we get home?"

"I live in London – I wouldn't have a home any more!"

"For goodness sake – Carol's crying!"

Meg held out her hand. "Come and pop in with me, Carol."

So Carol slid out of her bed and climbed in beside her.

"I'm homesick too," said Jayne, as she climbed in on the other side.

There was much shuffling around in the room, and soon all the beds were empty except two, and there were three in each of those. Crying and panic soon turned to giggling.

The door sprang open. Nurse MacLaren stood with the light behind her and stared at the empty beds; then at the occupied ones. She shrieked.

"Get out at once, all of you – and back to your own beds. Whatever will Mrs. Curtis think? You will all be severely punished in the morning. This is dreadful... really dreadful!"

Curty was summoned by phone the next day and the culprits stood in front of her to be lectured. She was wearing an enormous straw hat with a veil round the crown that tumbled down her back. Carol admired it very much, and only heard the end of the speech.

"So in view of the fact that you were feeling homesick after the long holiday at home, I will take no further action. But you must never, I repeat NEVER, behave like that again. Do you understand?"

The girls were closely watched after that. Even when they queued up each morning for their spoonful of cod liver oil and malt, Miss Kettle screwed up her eyes vindictively as she thrust the fishy, gluey spoonful into their mouths.

★ ★ ★

On 2 September 1945 World War Two came to an official end. But the Cold War was about to begin.

Carol's closest friend was Adrienne Fry and one day Adrienne asked her, "Are your parents divorced?" Carol was shocked.

"No, of course not."

She shrugged. "Mine are. Why do you think we have been sent to boarding school? It is to get us out of the way. They have to pretend to live normal lives when we are around, so with us safely at boarding school they can do exactly as they please."

Carol was devastated, but realised that it was almost certainly true.

After that, she became a rebel. She actually enjoyed behaving badly, being spiteful to the teachers, spoiling her written work, ignoring requests, hiding in the garden, feeling miserable. Perhaps if Mrs. Curtis had been living there, she might have disciplined her, but Nurse MacLaren and Miss Kettle found it easier to ignore rebellion than to try to quell it, so Carol felt increasing contempt for them both.

Carol spent two miserable terms at Newick, uplifted only when she sang *A Policeman's Lot is Not a Happy One* to rapturous applause from her school friends; and once again when the gaunt and unlovely Miss Kettle announced that she was engaged to be married!

Carol left Newick, and in 1946 arrived at Barcombe Mills station after a smoky journey through Uckfield and Titley, and walked down the road to Barcombe House.

It was square, rather Italianate in style, painted pink and white, with a small huddle of cottages and stables to the rear. These were the living quarters of the teachers, and the gardener, and where Matron governed the Sick bay, alias Punishment Block.

Curty had her private rooms on the first floor, above two of the schoolrooms and the huge music room. Big French windows with casement shutters opened out onto a magnificent terrace with stone balustrades and wide steps leading dramatically to the lush green lawn. In the distance, banks of rhododendron bushes concealed a winding footpath to the river. The dormitories and one other schoolroom were upstairs at the side of the house, with its own staircase leading down into the kitchen and dining room. The girls still had to queue each morning for their tablespoonful of malt, and Matron would ask each of them in turn: "Have you BEEN today?" and if they said "no" she gave them syrup of figs, and if they said "yes" she gave them kaolin and morphine.

There were fewer pianos for the twenty girls to share than at Eywood, but there were two grand pianos in the music room. Now that the school was accessible to London, Curty invited musicians down to give concerts nearly every week, some of them coming several times. Favourites were the Amadeus Quartet, charming rather elderly gentlemen, refugees who had managed to overcome their misfortunes and acquired enormous respect and appreciation.

Dennis Brain, the horn player and his brother Leonard thrilled them with their loudness, and Carol cruelly hoped that Dennis would "wobble" as he did in his famous 78 recording of the Mozart Horn Concerto. The Goosens family performed too, Leon the oboist and his sister Marie on her enormous gold harp.

Carol was particularly taken with Millicent Silver who played the harpsichord, accompanying her husband, John Francis, whose dexterity and tenderness on the flute convinced her that she wanted to learn to play that evocative instrument herself.

Curty took her pupils to Brighton for concerts, sending them by coach while she followed in her own little car. They heard the Vienna Boys Choir, and saw Benjamin Britten conduct Peter Pears and Dennis Brain in the Serenade for Tenor, Horn and Strings. For a special treat, Curty took Carol and another girl to a home for badly disabled children where the great pianist Dietrich Fischer Dieschau gave a charity concert for them. Carol must have been especially perverse to have received such a reward.

On Sundays they were all expected to go to church. The Roman Catholics went by car to Lewes, but the rest of the girls had to walk four miles to Ringmer. There was a perfectly good church just half a mile away in Barcombe village, but Curty had been told that it had been ravaged by the Plague in the fourteenth century, and she refused to risk her "gels" becoming contaminated.

Most of them however were afflicted with G.P. This stood for Grande Passion (French, of course) and Carol was not alone in adoring one of the older girls called Grizzy, following her around like a puppy, but unnoticed. Carol tried to sit near her in the library after supper when they crowded round the gramophone to listen to *Night on the Bare Mountain* in the dark. But someone else always got there first.

Grizzy, however, favoured one of Carol's friends, and they were discovered closeted together inside a wardrobe by Matron, and sent to the Sick bay in disgrace.

Music must have been the food of love, because the girls were not enamoured by their meals. Breakfast was lumpy porridge, salted instead of sweetened (Matron, after all, was a Scot). Lunch was chiefly one slice of corned beef, one jacket potato complete with eyes, well boiled cabbage or a slice of beetroot. This was followed by lumpy semolina. They could have a glass of freshly strained cabbage water to drink as well. Supper was sandwiches and a mug of cocoa made with hot water and a dash of milk. There were small variations to this diet, but food was still rationed and no doubt Matron and the cooks did their very best in the circumstances.

Curty had her meals in her room, her tray carried up by the ever-attentive Matron; a more appetising diet than the girls', perhaps a little chicken breast or tender white fish in mushroom sauce. Matron protected Curty from the wicked world, from contagious girls, hysterical parents, humiliated teachers and slovenly kitchen maids. Apparently Matron had been Curty's dresser during her professional opera singing days, and Matron still spent hours brushing Curty's long gold and silvery hair every night, and plaiting the neat round bun every morning. And no matter how busy Matron was, she still scurried to her mistress's side whenever she heard the strident call from the top of the stairs:

"Ma-Tron!"

Chapter Twelve
Flying Visit, 1946

During the summer term of 1946, Carol began to learn to play the flute. A little man from Brighton, Mr. Marriott, came twice a week to teach several of the girls, so Adrienne and Carol played duets together, part of a Brandenburg Concerto and other fairly simple pieces. Towards the end of term, Curty invited the parents to a concert in which nearly all her talented "gels" took part. Adrienne and Carol were due to start the second half with their duet, and in the interval Carol went to pick up their music, but it had disappeared. She searched in the dormitory, in the library, the study – panicking as Adrienne waited in front of the audience.

"Carry on then, dear," called Curty. Adrienne glanced desperately towards the door as the parents settled back into their seats. Carol stood in the doorway and burst into tears. "The music – I can't find it – it's vanished!" Adrienne pushed her outside, angry and ashamed. But Carol knew she would have to face her father after the concert; he had come all the way from Cambridge to share his daughter's moment of triumph.

It was worse than she thought – sitting beside her father she had spotted the elegant, gracious Mrs. Conway openly posing as her father's consort, and her presence filled Carol with misery. The following day was Sunday, and they came to Barcombe House and took her out for lunch in Lewes. Carol hardly spoke at all, while the doctor and Mrs. Conway made nervous small-talk and pretended they were quite at ease in her presence. It was a tremendous relief when they dropped Carol off at the gate.

Her mother had visited her at half term (this simply meant there were no lessons that particular Saturday morning), travelling down with Carol's godfather Bert Rumbelow and his wife Jimmy who had been living in Bottisham when Carol was born.

They drove to the coast at Seaford, where Carol refused to enjoy herself, sitting on the pebbles with her back to the sea. It was a very ungrateful way to behave, and it upset her mother and no doubt Bert and Jimmy as well. They were a very happy, comfortable couple, no children of their own, and with a very trusting outlook on life – whenever they went out for a meal or to the theatre with the Gilberts, somehow they always forgot to take any money.

★ ★ ★

The teachers at Barcombe were a motley crew. Mademoiselle who taught French suffered from a surfeit of blackheads so Carol nicknamed her "Strawberry Nose". There was the Commander who taught mathematics but preferred to recount his thrilling adventures in the Royal Navy. Carol hated arithmetic anyway, and bravely wrote to her father to beg him to allow her to give it up. After all, what use would maths be to an actress? Amazingly, he agreed, which is why Carol was never able to calculate the simplest sums, or give the correct change during her "resting" days behind the counter.

The real reason behind her anti-maths campaign was that she could not read the symbols and numbers written on the blackboard, unless she screwed up her eyes as tightly as possible. During the next holidays, Carol went to the cinema with her father and he watched in horror as she made a pinhole in a piece of paper and looked at the screen through this minute aperture.

As he was an eye specialist as well as a doctor, he tested her eyes as soon as they arrived home, and henceforth Carol had to wear dreadful spectacles on account of her astigmatism, whatever that was. The same thing as "stigma" probably, because now she was bespectacled as well as freckled, red-headed, bad-tempered, sulky and prone to chilblains. An unlovely child.

Happily, English was taught by Miss P. Green ("Pea Green") who breathed life and colour into the lengthiest poems of Wordsworth or Tennyson, and made grammar sensible and usable. The History teacher was Miss Marjorie Strachey, a close relative of Lytton Strachey. She had been a University lecturer before taking retirement and lowering herself to instil a genuine admiration for the chronicles of the past into a class of over-privileged, under-motivated adolescents.

There were at least three other teachers inhabiting the stable-block (except Pea Green who lived with her sister in a little house near the station), but only one deserves a mention. She was Italian, and like Carol she suffered terribly from chilblains, aggravated in those cold damp surroundings. But she had a splendid cure. At the end of the day, she would sit in her little room with her feet immersed in a chamber pot of warm fresh urine. Carol never tried it herself, but it must have been deliciously soothing.

★ ★ ★

Perhaps to make up for his earlier indiscretion, Dr. Gilbert came down again, on his own, at the end of term, having obtained Curty's permission to take Carol to Glyndebourne to see Benjamin Britten's new opera *The Rape of Lucretia* with the magnificent contralto Kathleen Ferrier playing the lead. He even brought her an evening dress to wear, white silk with pink and blue appliqué silk flowers all over it. The entire school gathered to watch Carol walk down the stairs to her waiting father, so handsome in his dinner suit, with Matron hovering by the front door, promising to wait up and let her in. It was a moment of indescribable delight.

During the War, John Christie's magnificent house at Glyndebourne had been used as a children's home, and this was the first performance at the opera house for seven years.

Everyone wore evening dress, and after the long first act with its stunning climax, they all wandered round the grounds, admiring the flower beds and the lake; and while most of the visitors laid rugs on the lawn and opened bulging picnic hampers, Carol and her father joined the rest in the dining room for a splendid meal.

In the final act, Kathleen Ferrier died magnificently, and the doctor took Carol back to school where Matron duly let her in. She tiptoed up to her dormitory, and her friends were instantly awake, demanding to know all the details, not so much about the elegant people, the opera house or the food, but how had they actually shown the rape itself? Carol explained that Kathleen Ferrier had been lying on the bed, with Tarquinius standing over her, fully clothed, and as he fell down on top of her, the lights went out and the curtains closed. Very disappointing.

The following morning, Carol's father took her home for the summer holidays. It was to be a memorable time.

First they went to visit kennels in Wilbraham to choose their new dog. There were six or seven squirming little fat Dalmatian puppies in a pen with their mother, and the owner lifted them out, one by one. Their faces were wrinkled and their noses were pink, and Carol would have kept them all. But somehow the decision was made, and they arranged to collect him a few weeks later.

Finding a name was difficult – it had to be suitable for a noble dog with an impressive pedigree, preferably Indian to link with his kennel name, Maharajah, and yet easy to call out in times of indiscipline. So he became Singhy, with a hard "j" sound.

He greeted their exchange holiday visitors, Bob and Janik Steenhaut, close relatives of their one-time Belgian guests. Bob immediately translated Singhy into "Singe" and called the poor dog "leetle monkey". He also complimented Carol on her small "tail", which after a hasty search in a dictionary revealed that he had referred to her twenty inch waist. The four became good friends, and spoke only English on the understanding that they all spoke only in French when they travelled back to Ghent.

Janik and Carol were fourteen and the boys sixteen, and Carol found Bob incredibly handsome – indeed, even more attractive than Grizzy.

The doctor drove them to London for their flight to Belgium. Only a year since the end of the War, passenger flights were still a novelty, and the only airport suitable was Croydon in South London, which had a couple of sheds as terminals, one with SABENA painted on the roof. Their plane was a large converted bomber, so it took off slowly and heavily, and lumbered through imaginary hills and valleys in the sky, turning their stomachs to jelly. The noise was deafening, a continual throbbing, and the journey was extremely long – but it was exhilarating.

M. and Mme. Steenhaut made them most welcome at Les Chaumes, in Destelbergen. Janik and Carol helped the maid with the washing-up, and Carol began to speak French more easily, picking up interesting slang phrases in the local dialect. One weekend the four of them, with two friends, went to Blankenberge, the most popular seaside resort in Belgium. They pedalled round the cobbled streets in curious machines, once going the wrong way up a one way street, until confronted by a solid policeman blocking their way who took Bob's name and address (both made up on the spot). Then they found a basement bar selling French fries, smothered in tangy sauces, before returning to their hotel which was run by an uncle of Bob's, where they drank something very sweet in the private bar. David got very drunk.

They spent the last few days cycling along the narrow flat roadways, or playing table tennis. The evening before her father came to take them home, Carol crept away and hid in a shed, feeling utterly miserable. She was there for two hours before M. Steenhaut found her, much to everyone's relief as they had been calling and searching, even wading into the shallow boating lake fearing that she had fallen in. Carol did not want to leave Belgium, to have to return to that atmosphere of forced politeness between her parents, which she and David had learnt to ignore but which nonetheless hurt them deeply. They would be treading on egg-shells, being careful whenever they spoke, pretending not to notice their father's fingers drumming on the dining table just before the phone would ring and he would hurry into his consulting room to answer it.

So they went home, and shortly back to school. Autumn term at Langford Grove passed rapidly, with concerts in the music room, *Comic Cuts* for visiting parents, painting lessons by the river, walks across the fields to place coins on the railway line to be squashed flat by the next train, and a coach trip to Brighton for a concert in the Dome.

In November the pupils went by train to Lewes to watch the extraordinary annual Tar Barrel Rolling that marks Guy Fawkes Day. The burning barrels are prodded with sticks from the highest point in the town, until they roll with ever increasing speed through the streets and down to the river, accompanied by cheering crowds carrying lighted firebrands and setting off fireworks. It was a marvellous excuse that year for people to be thoroughly noisy and carefree, so soon after the miseries of the War.

★ ★ ★

The girls' education continued its unusual progress. Someone found a copy of D.H. Lawrence's *Lady Chatterley's Lover* in the library, the early unexpurgated version, so certain passages were heavily marked and they took it in turns to learn more about sex.

Unfortunately, Matron caught one of the girls red-handed, and the book was confiscated. At least it had taught them that reading was a worthwhile chore, and they worked their way through shelves of fiction and biographies searching for knowledge.

Annabel was rather bored with this, so she found some matches and set fire to the library armchair. Smoke poured into the room and while someone threw cups of water over the chair, Annabel was sent to the Sick bay in disgrace. Curty summoned her to her room the next day, and they were closeted together for a long time. Everyone expected an imminent sending down, but instead Annabel was reprieved because her action, according to Curty, while wrong, showed that she had an independent, creative, flair and unique imagination, which was to be encouraged.

★ ★ ★

One evening, while Matron was busy and out of earshot, six girls decided to play Planchette. They wrote the letters of the alphabet on small pieces of paper, laid them all round the edge of a table, and placed an upturned glass in the centre. They each rested one finger on the glass and waited.

"Is there anybody there?" somebody asked. "One knock for yes, two knocks for no," and the glass tipped briefly.

"Who are you?" The glass began to move, touching several letters and spelling a word - "GRAN".

"Whose Gran?" It moved again, and spelt "CAROL". Carol sat back in alarm.

"You've spoilt it now," they complained, so she went and sat in the corner. Through the window she could see the moon. It was a strange colour, almost red.

"It's blood on the moon," Adrienne said. "It means someone is going to die."

Two days later Carol received a letter from her mother breaking the sad news that Granny Ennion had passed away. She shivered at the thought that Granny had perhaps been trying to contact her as she died, but yet it seemed reassuring. She never told her mother, but she would have understood.

★ ★ ★

For her fifteenth birthday on 14 December, her mother sent her a large pink and white birthday cake. She concealed it in her wardrobe, and planned a special midnight feast in the rickety boathouse by the river. But rather than catch cold in their pyjamas, the girls decided to wait until six o'clock that morning, and a group of them dressed and put on their coats, crept downstairs and let themselves out into the garden.

It was a delicious cake. When they returned, breakfast was nearly ready, and Matron smiled with unusual warmth, insisting that each girl had an extra helping of porridge. Later Carol's friends made her walk backwards down the stairs, with her mouth full of water, gargling *Happy Birthday*.

★ ★ ★

When the doctor came to meet her in London at the end of term, he told her that her cat Mrs. Perkins had been put to sleep, so tired and thin after producing so many kittens. He had taken the sad decision out of kindness, but Carol was heartbroken. There was no excited fluffy grey bundle waiting for her when she arrived home, no warm body nestling at her side every night, throbbing rhythmically even when asleep. Singhy did his best to take her place, but he loved Mrs. Gilbert more than he loved Carol, while Mrs. Perkins had always been her very own special friend.

Chapter Thirteen
Enter Stage Right, 1947 And Beyond

The first few weeks of 1947 were bitter – the girls shivered in their unheated dormitories and classrooms as snow fell in thick lumps, filling the lanes and fields with sculptured snowdrifts. They wondered when the local tradesmen would be able to reach the school and bring much needed supplies. They were at least excused the long walk to Ringmer church on Sundays. To pass the time they wrote plays and acted them, created string quartets and woodwind quintets, painted and drew, and even studied for the forthcoming School Certificate exams in the spring.

But spring brought extensive floods after the big thaw. Most of East Anglia and much of Barcombe Mills was under water. They had to wade from the station carrying their shoes and socks while their luggage was transported to the school by tractor. The school cesspit became contaminated, and most of the girls contracted fearsome sore throats; Carol's was the worst, clogged with big septic spots. Her temperature rose to 104, and when her father arrived and drove her home, she was virtually unconscious on the back seat.

Consequently she missed the School Cert exams, but she was allowed to sit them the following term, and the gentleman who came especially to test her oral French was most impressed with her fluency, with its Belgian variations and colloquial phrases. Her best results were French,

English and Art, but somehow the History papers went missing and she needed them to qualify. Happily the Oxford and Cambridge Examinations Board decided to give her the benefit of the doubt, and granted her School Certificate. Later the History papers magically appeared, and were marked so low that she ought to have failed.

★ ★ ★

In June, Kathleen Ferrier returned to Glyndebourne for Gluck's beautiful opera *Orfeo*. Curty obtained permission from the producer for a party of "gels" to attend a rehearsal in the opera house. Matron was put in charge of them, and they sat enthralled in the auditorium as Miss Ferrier sang *Che Faro* two or three times while the stage lighting was adjusted. In the middle of a quiet, poignant phrase, a loud snort reverberated from the back row. Everyone, including Miss Ferrier, peered into the gloom to see Matron, head thrown back, eyes closed, mouth wide open, fast asleep and snoring. They were acutely embarrassed.

Concert performers came again to Barcombe Mills, and famous parents collected their daughters for rare moments of bonding. One evening Carol leant out of a dormitory window to see the actor Robert Newton pulling up in a pony and trap to collect his Russian niece, Tanya, his ruddy complexion, blood-shot eyes and exuberant manner so familiar from the film version of *Treasure Island*.

That summer, Carol went again to Belgium and found Bob just as attractive, but he seemed rather cool towards her. She expressed her disappointment in the usual way, by sulking, refusing to help Janik with the washing-up, refusing to speak French, and generally making herself disagreeable. No wonder Bob preferred Monique.

Her confidence was greatly restored, however, when Peter Knee, David's old school friend, invited her to tea at the Strand Palace Hotel in London. Peter was serving in the

Navy aboard HMS President moored on the Thames, and he met her at Liverpool Street Station, in his smart uniform. They had a happy day, comfortable in each other's company, so they lingered rather too long over the buttered teacakes.

"We shall have to hurry to catch that train," said Peter, and they rushed to the nearest underground station and down through the crowds to the tube. Suddenly Carol felt something ping on her left leg – one of her suspenders had come undone. Each stocking was held up by two suspenders so she was not too concerned. As they pushed their way onto the escalator she felt the second one go, and then both on the other side. Appalled, she tried to hurry, grasping the top of each stocking through her dress, but in vain. They began to roll down her legs and clung around her ankles. She just wanted to die on the spot. Peter glanced down, then at her stricken face.

"Oh Lord!" he sighed, and grabbed her by the elbow and physically thrust her onto the train. As it pulled away he did grin at her, and wave, but he never asked her out again.

★ ★ ★

Carol's last few months at Barcombe Mills with Langford Grove were tinged with sadness, knowing they were all soon to part. However they were almost grown up so they agreed to explore the world outside and face whatever it should offer. Four girls decided to go to Brighton one Saturday morning, so they sneaked out through the back garden and walked up to the main road. As usual Carol's feet were sore, so the other two set off ahead. Annabel and Carol kept their thumbs crooked as the cars passed, and saw one slow down to pick up their friends. Then another car braked and stopped just in front of them, so they ran up to it, wreathed in smiles.

"And just where did you think you were going?" snapped Curty from the driver's seat. She drove them straight back to school. The others had a marvellous time, exploring the shops, trying on clothes, and were even chatted up by two young men in a café. Curty was waiting for them when they rolled in just before dark.

★ ★ ★

The girls talked about the future – some of Carol's friends were hoping to go to University, and a few were talking excitedly about coming-out parties (this meant coming out into Society, not as in the current usage of the words), and being presented to the King. The talented musicians would join orchestras, or become music teachers, but Carol could only mimic other people and act the fool, according to her brother; he was soon to enter Trinity College to study law, but Carol's future was still undecided. She only wanted to become an actress.

However, her father decided that she was still in need of further education, so she was enrolled at the Perse School for Girls in Cambridge, as a By-student. That meant that she was not taking the entire Higher Certificate course, attending the school only part-time.

Far more agreeably, twice a week Mrs. Kay Barrow called to see Carol at Bottisham to give her lessons in speech and drama. She was an energetic, colourful woman, who managed to drive her small car with ferocity despite having one stiff leg, due to TB. She had agreed to train Carol to enter the Guildhall School of Music and Drama in London. Carol had to learn poems, and short scenes from well-known plays, taking two parts and changing her voice and stance to define each character. These were chiefly for the entrance audition.

Kay took Carol up to London that auspicious day, and she walked into the Guildhall School for the first time. The entrance hall had a waiting room built under the massive stairwell, and they sat and watched students carrying violin cases, play-scripts, even fencing equipment, embracing each other, hurrying down to the basement toilets and the drama rehearsal rooms, or up the stairs to the dozens of music practice rooms encircling the galleries, or going into the theatre on the ground floor.

Kay and Carol went up in a tiny lift controlled by a polite uniformed man with only one arm. Soon Carol was standing before Guy Pertwee, one of the drama teachers, who guided her through the audition. He asked her various personal questions, watched her set pieces, and then told her to perform a mime on an unrehearsed subject. Of course Carol had been practising one that would hopefully fit anything from *The Lost Purse* to *Journey on a Train* and managed to give a reasonable performance.

Several weeks later Kay rang to say that Carol had been accepted, and could start a three-year acting course in September 1949.

Bo Mann, her friend Helen's brother, had suggested that Carol contact him once she had left school, with a view to joining his orchestra in Cambridge. He was the conductor of CUMS (Cambridge University Musical Society) and he also coached less proficient performers in the CUMS Junior orchestra. So Carol became sixth flute and attended rehearsals every week. The string section had fewer members than the woodwind, but Bo was an energetic conductor and somehow they managed to give reasonable renditions of familiar pieces by Elgar, Brahms and Beethoven. Carol's inability to read music was unnoticed however, except by the boy who played fifth flute beside her, and he taught her to play by ear. Otherwise she had to count the lines and spaces between the black dots and sing the difference in her head before actually playing what she hoped was the right note. This was quite satisfactory until one terrible rehearsal when four of the flautists failed to turn up. Carol was promoted to second flute. They were to play Beethoven's Seventh Symphony in which there is a section where first and second flute play a duet, then the second flute carries on for a few bars on its own. They reached this section, and as the duet ended, Bo nodded towards Carol. There was sudden complete silence. Bo tapped his baton on the music stand.

"Come on, Carol – this is your big moment. One – two – and..." Nothing.

Carol burst into tears and ran out of the room. Bitterly ashamed, she had to confess her problem to Bo, which amused him greatly, but obviously he could not keep her in the orchestra.

★ ★ ★

At least her acting career was to be safely launched. She joined the Cambridge Theatre Group, run by Mrs. Camille Prior at her home, 8 Scroope Terrace, where a motley collection of members, college professors, gentlemen farmers, office girls and at least one frightfully gay chap, held weekly play readings. Some of these led to rehearsals and eventually performances at the ADC Theatre, and occasionally in college gardens. One such production was a variety show entitled *Hey Nonny No*, and the cast had to sing various naughty songs and act wicked sketches that had to be explained to Carol. It was great fun.

Joan Hopkins had been one of Kay Barrow's early pupils, and when the Gilberts heard that she was appearing at the Arts Theatre, they invited her to spend the final weekend at Beaulieu House. She was delightful, not a bit "theatrical", but full of fun and as pleased as Carol was when everyone remarked on their striking resemblance to each other.

★ ★ ★

The doctor insisted that even the most accomplished actress encounters periods of "rest" when she might need to take on a temporary job, perhaps in an office, so early in 1949 he enrolled her into a small secretarial establishment in a private house in Station Road to learn shorthand and typing. The teacher was a careworn mousey little spinster, who put on the kettle for tea just before 4.15 each day, so that she could listen to Mrs. Dale's Diary. There were only five in the class, and they all managed to learn to type with some accuracy, but Carol never mastered shorthand. However the typing proved to be immensely useful, as her father had predicted.

★ ★ ★

In the spring of 1949, several of her Theatre Group colleagues invited Carol to join them for a special production with the BATS. Every May Week (which incidentally is always in June) the members of BATS perform a play by Shakespeare, immaculately costumed, in the magnificent black and white cloister of Queens' College. They appeared in *All's Well that Ends Well* but it nearly became *All's Well that Ends in the Middle* when one of the leading ladies fainted in the heat, burdened by a tight bodice beneath several petticoats and a heavy velvet gown.

Those two years between leaving boarding school and entering college were filled with all these stimulating activities – playing in an orchestra, having speech and drama tuition, learning shorthand and typing, joining the Theatre Group and appearing in plays, as well as attending the Perse School, infrequently, and learning absolutely nothing.

But they were also noteworthy for a catalogue of fleeting love affairs. There were one or two exciting moments climbing out of college windows after midnight to avoid being seen by the Porters. There were lazy days in a punt on the Cam; two May Balls in one week with rival undergraduates; one salutary evening after a party reeling down the middle of Market Street when a taxi stopped beside Carol and the driver said, "I think I ought to take you home!"

Her heart was broken several times, by charming young men recently demobbed from the RAF or the Army, but the majority had arrived at Cambridge straight from school.

★ ★ ★

As Carol started her new life at the Guildhall School, her mother acknowledged that now both David and Carol had left home, she had no further excuse to remain either. The doctor was still openly accompanying Mrs. Conway to restaurants and parties, so Ruth's best friend Margery Turner convinced her that she must leave and begin divorce proceedings.

A kind professor lent her his house, The Grove at Newnham, and within weeks she accepted two foreign students into her temporary home. She created a special bedroom for Carol, and one for David, and they spent their holidays there, with weekends at Bottisham with their father.

A private detective was able to collect enough evidence for the divorce proceedings to begin. The case was heard in London, the decree was given, and the marriage was over.

Singhy left with Mrs. Gilbert, despite the doctor's protests. He even took her to Court to regain possession of "his" dog. The local policeman was called as a witness for the defence, and his evidence was unshakeable:

"Sometimes that dog escaped and was to be found in a nearby farmer's chicken run. I would ring the doctor and tell him to fetch his dog back. He would always say, "He's not my dog, he's my wife's dog. Tell her to bring him home!" So Singhy remained with Mrs. Gilbert.

The doctor made an agreement through solicitors that he would give his ex-wife a certain sum of money to enable her to buy a house, with an additional two lump sums that he had intended to give David and Carol on their twenty-first birthdays. So the house she bought, 70 Gilbert Road, belonged to the three of them for the next thirty years. Mrs. Gilbert arranged with the new Language Schools to have three or four foreign students living with her on full-board. Carol met many of them during her weekend visits and holidays, and it was gratifying to see how much her mother was enjoying her new life. She had taught herself to cook incredibly delicious meals and the girls loved her. One was to become the Queen of Norway, and another married David.

★ ★ ★

The Ennions uprooted themselves once more, from Flatford Mill to Seahouses in Northumberland, to open a new bird observatory at Monks House virtually on the beach. Carol spent a few days there, helping Aunt Dorothy with the bed making and cutting vast piles of sandwiches for the keen students. Her Uncle encouraged them to get up at the crack of dawn, to check the drift nets, and other nets on the cliffs, to ring the captive birds before releasing them as soon as possible. They went batfowling at dusk to catch starlings, shooing them into wide nets before ringing and sexing them and flinging them back into the darkness.

As an ignorant non-twitcher it was a memorable experience. One morning Carol saw through the living room window a black and white bird strutting along the beach. She shouted:

"Look! There's a penguin!" and they all rushed excitedly forward, focussing their binoculars, whooping with delight. By the time they had realised that it was only a common oyster catcher, Carol was hiding in the laundry cupboard.

★ ★ ★

After the divorce, the doctor suggested to Mrs. Conway that she should also start divorce proceedings, so they could eventually marry. But she prevaricated, finding good excuses not to end one marriage just to enter another.

The doctor decided to holiday in Switzerland on his own, to renew the acquaintance of Dr. Weder and his charming wife Vroni, whom he had met some years before at an international medical conference. Arriving at the address they had given him, he was astounded to be greeted by a brand new Mrs. Weder. Undaunted, he managed to discover the whereabouts of Vroni and her daughter Beatrice, and immediately went to find them.

Their friendship blossomed, and a few months later, the doctor asked Vroni to marry him and she accepted. So now he had the difficult task of breaking this news to Mrs. Conway. He chose to tell her when David was there, visiting Beaulieu House against his will. No doubt the doctor insisted that he should be present, knowing he was about to drop a devastating bomb-shell. How would she react, being cast aside by her lover of nearly ten years, for a new and younger model?

She flew at him in a rage, clutched at his tie and pulled it as tight as she could. David grabbed her, and managed to pull her away, but the doctor was gasping for air, the tie slowly choking him to death. Somehow David found some scissors and cut through the tie, and as the doctor collapsed into a chair, David dragged Mrs. Conway out into the hall, opened the door and pushed her out. The doctor recovered soon enough, but it is doubtful if she ever forgave him.

A few days later, the doctor called to see his ex-wife at Gilbert Road – his first and only visit – and to her surprise and utter confusion, he asked her for her blessing for his forthcoming marriage to Vroni. Stunned, she gave it and he left wreathed in smiles.

They were married at Cambridge Register office at the Shire Hall, and set up house in Bottisham, with little Beatrice going daily to school in Cambridge. She and Carol became very attached to each other. Some years later, the doctor decided to retire to Switzerland, and he sold Beaulieu House and the practice to Dr. Silverston, founder of the excellent voluntary medical care service in Cambridgeshire, MAGPAS.

★ ★ ★

Leaving home and going to Drama School somehow closed the early chapters of Carol's life. But she did go back to Bottisham, in 1989, for Maurice and Katie Coleman's Golden Wedding. Nursie had managed to contact her through a distant cousin in Soham, so after forty-five years they were reunited. The reception was held at Anglesey Abbey tea rooms for eighty guests; Carol wore her little gold bracelet and to everyone's delight the other bridesmaid was wearing hers too. Maurice proudly wore the same suit in which he had been married fifty years before.

Carol stayed the night with Mary Green, the new owner of Towler's Farm just across the road from Beaulieu House. Most of the camp Nissen huts and concrete buildings had been demolished in the meadow next door, but close to the house there was a new housing estate. The single roadway bore the name "Thomas Christian Close" and at the entrance Carol saw a memorial stone with this inscription:

"The street is situated on what was part of Bottisham Air Base, and is named in honour of Colonel Thomas J. Christian Jnr., Commander of the 361st Fighter Group, 8th Air Force who with members of his command flew from here and gave his life in defence of freedom during World War II."

It had been unveiled on 6 October 1988 by his daughter, Mrs. Lou Christian Wilson Fleming, and Carol wished she had been there.

The old house looked much the same, but she turned away and walked up the road, past the row of white cottages, and Granny Ennion's last home. The thatched cottage and Dummy's shed had gone from the grassy triangle at the junction of Swaffham Road and Lode Road, but the Bell Inn was still there.

Further up the main street, Bedford's store had become a restaurant, and beyond the church there was a cluster of new roads lined with fashionable semis. At the top end of the village Carol discovered that Graham Brown's old house, The Grange, next to the White Swan, had become a retirement home. All the traffic had been transferred away from the village onto a new motorway which had been laid on the concrete landing strip built by the RAF.

Carol bravely knocked on Mr. Paul's farmhouse door, and Betty Paul invited her in. They chatted about the old days, and after a while Betty went outside and Carol heard her calling:

"Bernard! Come and see who's turned up after all these years!"

A tall man in his late fifties stood in the doorway, staring at her.

"Why, if it isn't Miss Carol!"

Bernard, her first playmate, Wisbech's little boy who had let her sit on his lap on her swing, and helped to dig up the tennis court, and collected chucky eggs with her in the orchard. Bernard.

They smiled shyly at each, and shook hands. Then Carol turned and walked away, back through the village, as her eyes filled with tears.

Postscript – The Return, 2005

In October 2005, Carol was invited to give a talk to the members of Bottisham W.I. and was taken to meet the present owners of Beaulieu House. This is the poem she wrote after her visit:

THE RETURN

I got off the bus by the old village green
Just as I did after school years ago.
I walked down the lane where the cottage had been,
Recalling the people that I used to know.

    There in her garden is old Mrs. Shaw,
    In her slippers and pinny and big friendly smile,
    So proud of her son taking part in the War.
    "Tell your mother, Miss Carol, I'll be there in a while
    And scramble some eggs for your supper tonight!"
    She helps in the kitchen since Cook joined the WRENS,
    As my mother can't cook, this put us in a plight.
    Even I have to help, by feeding the hens.
    Although food is rationed in all of the shops,
    We eat very well if the patients are ill,
    'Cos they bring us their fruit, and bacon and chops
    Instead of paying the Doctor's bill!"

I stood in the drive leading up to my home,
It didn't seem to have changed at all,
Then I noticed the walls at the entrance had gone,
With the pillars atopped by a big concrete ball.

"The huge tank is swerving and, look! It's destroyed
Our gatepost, and broken bricks lie on the ground.
"Pick it up!" shouts my father; he's very annoyed!
And the man in the tank climbs onto the ground.
He picks up the pieces and builds it again,
Then he turns to my father and gives a salute,
Gets back in his tank and goes off down the lane,
With me and evacuees in hot pursuit."

I walked up to the door, my heart hardly beating,
But I knocked. Said the lady "I'm so glad you came!
We've made a few changes – we've got central heating,
The surgery's gone but the rest's much the same."
She showed me the kitchen, the lounge and upstairs,
The bedrooms, the attic, new windows and wall.
And although I could see what they'd changed through the
        years
In my heart my old home hadn't altered at all.

Someone is crying. It must be my mother.
It's dark in the attic so she's holding my hand.
My father's here too and so is my brother,
Silently staring out over the land.
A glow in the sky is weaving and turning
From orange to scarlet and shining like day.
There in the distance London is burning,
We watch it, though we're fifty miles away."

"Please, do come down for a nice cup of tea!
My daughter is dying to meet you," she says!
So we sat on settees, and they all stared at me
As I spoke of those wonderful, childhood days -
How I hid in the kennel with my faithful dog,
How we stored bags of sweets in the old tree house,
How I'd capture and try to re-home every frog,

How I scooped up the hens feed and found a brown mouse,
How I toppled when small in the new swimming pool,
How we crawled round the attic all under the eaves,
How I wetted my pants on my first day at school,
How we walked in the Park and kicked up the leaves.

The daughter was smiling and sat by my side.
"I know you," she said, "I'm so glad you are here.
I know all the places where you used to hide,
Because when I pass them I feel someone near,
And sometimes I catch a glimpse at the most
Of a red-headed girl - and then she is gone.
But at last I am seeing my dear little ghost.
Welcome back home! This is where you belong!"

THE MILESTONES AND ALL THOSE WHO SHARED IN THE JOURNEY

A

Albert, Prince de Ligne
The Amadeus Quartet

B

Kay Barrow
Marguerite de Beaumont
Bedford Stores,
Bottisham
Sally Bicknell
Bottisham LDV, Home
Guard
Bottisham Village College
Benjamin Britten
The Brown family
MissBeryl Burns
Byron House School

C

Cambridge Theatre
Group
Hubert Casin
Neville Chamberlain
Michael Chapman
Charles I
Colonel Christian
John Christie
Winston Churchill
The Coleman family
The Conway family
Mrs Cornwall

Barry Craig R.A.
Elizabeth Curtis

D

Lady Darwin
Frances Day
Dietrich Fischer
Dieschau
Doris the maid
Madeleine Z. Doty
Ruth Draper
"Dummy"
Isadora Duncan

E

The Ennion family

F

Kathleen Ferrier
James Fisher
Sir Alexander Fleming
John Francis
Adrienne Fry

G

George V Jubilee
George VI
Gertie the maid
The Gilbert family
Pilot Officer Ginn
Glyndebourne Opera

Leon and Marie
Goossens
Mary Green
Miss Phyllis Green
Joyce Grenfell
Guildhall School of
Music and Drama

H

Anne Harris
Miss Henderson
Dame Myra Hess
Rowland Hilder
Adolf Hitler
Frances Hodgkins
Joan Hopkins
Olive Howard
Mrs Howlett
Anthea Hume

J

Mrs. Jenyns
Kurt and Anna Jooss

K

Miss Kettle
Peter Knee

L

Langford Grove School
Mr Leder
The Lwowski family

M

Nurse Maclaren

John McCormack
Bo and Helen Mann
Ambrose Marriott
Arthur Marshall
Mrs. Millard

N

Robert Newton
Ben Nicholson

P

Paderewski
Mrs. Pankhurst
Mr.Paul, A.R.P
Betty Paul
Peter Pears
Loughnan and Dulcie
Pendred
Mrs Pethick-Laurence
Mrs. Pettit
Freddie Potter
Sq.Leader Harold Pound
J.B.Priestley
Sally Prince
Camille Prior
John Profumo M.P.

R

Miss Randall
Rawicz and Landauer
Frank Reeve
Bouverie Roberts
Waldon T. Ross USAAF
Capt. Bert Rumbelow
Mrs. Jimmy Rumbelow

Lindy Runcie, née
Turner
Rev. and Mrs Harry
Russell
Joan Russell

S

The Silbermann family
Dr. Silverston
Millicent Silver
Sonja, Queen of Norway
St. Colette's School
Miss Natalie Starr
The Steenhaut family
Miss Stephens
Lytton Strachey
Marjorie Strachey

T

Mrs. Thornley
Madge Towler
The Turner family

U

"Uncle Mac"
Rev. Canon Uthwatt

W

Roy Webb, USAAF
The Weder family
Mrs. Lou Christian
Wilson-Fleming
Dr. Wood
Arthur Wisbech
Bernard Wisbech
Violet Wisbech